ASHES 2010–11

THE AMAZING STORY OF ENGLAND'S TRIUMPH DOWN UNDER

First published in 2011 by
Carlton Books Limited
20 Mortimer Street
London W1T 3JW

10 9 8 7 6 5 4 3 2 1

A CIP catalogue record for this book is available from the British Library.

The publisher has taken reasonable steps to check the accuracy of the facts contained herein at the time of going to press, but can take no responsibility for any errors.

ISBN: 978-1-84732-851-9

Printed in the United Kingdom
by Butler Tanner & Dennis, Frome

Press Association Sport
Chief writer: Chris Devine
Contributors: David Clough, Dominic Farrell, Matthew Sherry, Jonathan Veal
Head of content: Peter Marshall
Copy editor: Andrew McDermott
2010–11 photography: Gareth Copley/Press Association Images
Archive photography: AP/PA Photographs (page 7)
Design: Mark Tattersall

Press Association Sport is the official compiler of the ECB cricket record and works closely with the ECB and the English Professional Cricketers' Association, providing data, statistics and editorial content.

ASHES
2010–11

THE AMAZING STORY OF ENGLAND'S TRIUMPH DOWN UNDER

CARLTON

Contents

Foreword by Mike Gatting, OBE

There is something very special about the Ashes. The whole country seems to go cricket mad whenever England and Australia meet on the cricket field and the 2010–11 series in Australia certainly lived up to expectations from an England point of view. Winning the Ashes was one of the highlights of my career and doing so Down Under, as Andrew Strauss has done, is as good as it gets. It is hard to believe that my team's glory was 24 years ago.

Cricket has a wonderful way of throwing up characters and making heroes out of the most unexpected players. Who, after all, would have thought that Chris Tremlett, out of the England limelight for three and a half years, would take 17 wickets in three Tests after Stuart Broad broke down; or that Tim Bresnan would take 11 wickets in two Tests after replacing Steven Finn, who until then had been the series' leading wicket-taker.

We all knew that Australia were in rebuilding mode, but they were like that in 1986, when I could count on David Gower, Ian Botham, Chris Broad, Allan Lamb, John Emburey, Phil Edmonds, Gladstone Small and Graham Dilley. We had some real characters in the team, and I remember after some poor performances in the warm-up matches, one journalist wrote that we were weaker than Australia in only three departments: batting, bowling and fielding. Well we won the series 2–1, and took the two one-day series into the bargain!

The 2010–11 Test matches will live long in the memory and reading about them brought a smile to this proud Englishman's face. I hope you enjoy this glorious illustrated book as much as I did.

I suppose the highlight of the recent Ashes series for me was the way that the batsmen took complete control from the opening match. To score 517–1 in the second innings in Brisbane was an incredible achievement, in particular Alastair Cook's unbeaten 235, and, less than a

6

week later, to rack up 620–5 was remarkable. Having scored all those runs, it was important for the bowlers to take wickets, and all six front-line bowlers made telling contributions in at least one innings.

Winning the second Test match in Adelaide was so important, because as we were holders of the Ashes, the Aussies had to win at least two of the last three Tests, and they had too many players who were out of touch to have a real chance. Graeme Swann was magnificent in the second innings and his five-for destroyed Australia on the final morning, just before the predicted bad weather hit.

After losing on the trampoline of a pitch at Perth, the one time the batting failed to deliver, the Ashes were back in the melting-pot, but the Andys – Strauss and Flower – didn't panic and things got back on track at Melbourne. To retain the Ashes with a match to go was fantastic and to really rub the Aussies' noses in it in Sydney was the icing on the cake.

The Ashes are always keenly contested but the team captains are usually happy to share a post-match beer, as Allan Border and Mike Gatting show here in 1987.

"These Test matches will live long in the memory and reading about them brought a smile to this proud Englishman's face. I hope you enjoy this glorious illustrated book as much as I did."
MIKE GATTING, OBE

Introduction

Many people believed that England were capable of winning the Ashes as they headed Down Under for the 2010–11 series, but few could have imagined that, in doing so, they would heap so much pain on their oldest cricketing rivals. Australia had reigned supreme on their home soil for more than two decades, dishing out a series of punishing beatings in the process, but on this occasion they would suffer a bitter taste of their own medicine.

As the 2010–11 Ashes drew to a close in Sydney, there was a familiar feeling to proceedings.

In keeping with many of England's previous series in Australia, one team had displayed almost total dominance throughout and were about to wrap up another comprehensive triumph. However, on this occasion, it was the tourists who were handing out the punishment.

For the first time in 24 years, England would return from the Antipodes with the famous little urn in their grasp and the manner of their success could not have been more emphatic.

Following the drawn series-opener at the Gabba, which saw Andrew Strauss declare his side's second innings on the scarcely believable score of 517 for one, England surged to innings victories in three of the four remaining Tests, with a heavy defeat in Perth their only setback.

By the time that proceedings were brought to a close at the Sydney Cricket Ground, Australia were in disarray, with players and selectors alike facing widespread criticism.

It was no surprise to see skipper Ricky Ponting, who missed the final Test with a broken finger, coming under particularly heavy fire and, after a poor series with the bat, it remained to be seen whether he would lead his country again in the premier form of the game. England, by contrast, were able to revel in the satisfaction of a job well done, having exceeded all expectations with a number of outstanding performances. Each and every player contributed to the team's success, while certain individuals took their game to new heights.

Chief among these was Alastair Cook, who claimed the Compton-Miller medal for the man of the series. The opener's credentials had been doubted in the build-up to the tour, but he answered his critics in stunning fashion by compiling a staggering 766 runs at an average of 128.

Cook was the undoubted star of a batting line-up that posted scores in excess of 500 in four of the five Tests, yet the efforts of England's bowlers were no less impressive.

Spearheaded by the outstanding James Anderson, the only member of the attack to have previously featured in Tests on Australian soil, they demonstrated great skill and discipline to restrict their hosts to a succession of below-par totals.

Fittingly, England's most comprehensive victory arrived on the biggest stage of all as they romped to an innings-and-157-run win in the Boxing Day Test in Melbourne. Australia went into that match in buoyant mood following their success in Perth, but their confidence soon suffered a mortal blow as they were dismissed for a paltry 98 on day one.

It would prove to be the final shift in momentum in an engrossing series, with Ponting's men unable to stage another fightback.

The Ashes are held in a 5½-inch-high, 129-year-old terracotta urn which has become one of the most iconic trophies in the world of sport.

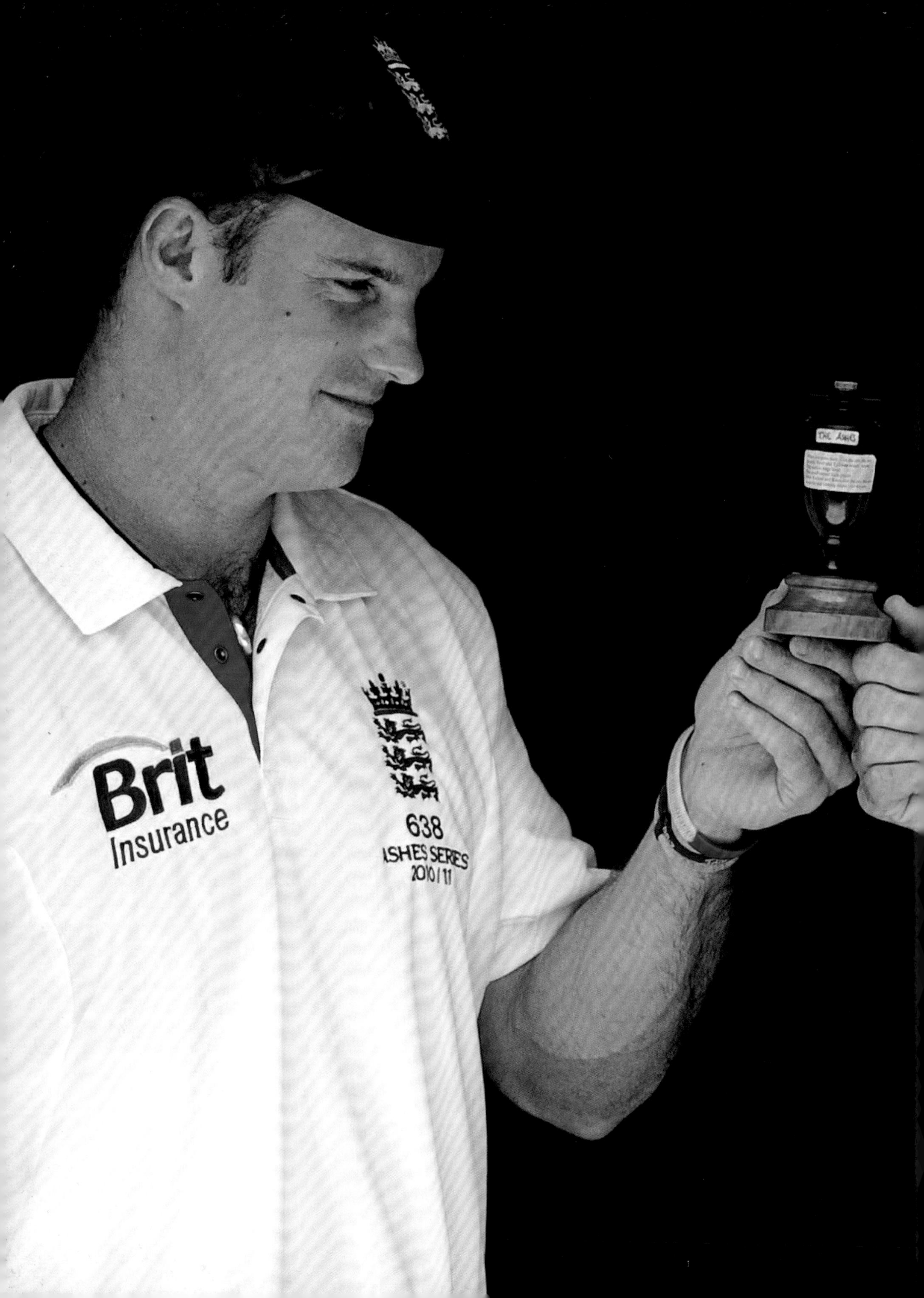
Brit
Insurance
638
ASHES SERIES
2010/11

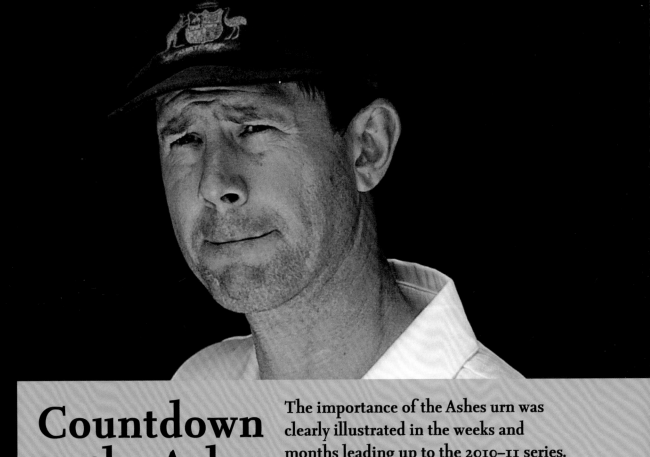

Countdown to the Ashes

The importance of the Ashes urn was clearly illustrated in the weeks and months leading up to the 2010–11 series. For captains Andrew Strauss and Ricky Ponting, anything less than victory would represent a crushing setback. It was no surprise, therefore, to see their teams coming under intense scrutiny as the first Test in Brisbane approached.

Ashes 2010/11
366

1

Countdown to the Ashes

England and Australia experienced mixed fortunes in the build-up to the 2010–11 Ashes. The tourists were in good form and their preparation could hardly have gone more smoothly, but there was growing uncertainty over the make-up of a faltering Australia side that had suffered a host of confidence-denting defeats.

The tone had been set for England's Ashes defence before the squad had even landed in Australia.

In his final press conference ahead of England's departure, team director Andy Flower spoke with a quiet confidence that would come to be a hallmark of his side throughout the winter.

Never a man to waste his words, Flower calmly explained: "We respect the opposition but we don't fear them. I don't think there's anything to be afraid of. It's actually a tour that should be welcomed."

England's players certainly seemed to be in good spirits from the moment they touched down in Perth at the end of October and they had every reason to be optimistic given their impressive form.

After defeating Australia in the final of the World Twenty20 to claim their first major ICC trophy, England enjoyed a relatively comfortable summer as they came out on top in Test and limited-overs series against Bangladesh and Pakistan. They also enjoyed success over their oldest rivals in the NatWest Series, winning the first three matches before Australia hit back in the final two games.

Defeats were to become increasingly common for Ricky Ponting's men and a 2-0 reverse at the hands of India in October ensured that they would head into the Ashes on the back of three straight Test losses. The skipper was coming under increasing pressure as a result, while the likes of Mike Hussey, Marcus North and Nathan Hauritz appeared to be facing a battle to hold on to their places.

England were far more settled and fielded their first-choice XI in their opening three-day game against Western Australia, with Steven Finn earning the final bowling slot alongside James Anderson, Stuart Broad and Graeme Swann.

Both Flower and captain Andrew Strauss had highlighted the need to take the warm-up matches seriously and the team responded admirably with a professional display that saw them claim victory by six wickets.

"We respect the opposition but we don't fear them. I don't think there's anything to be afraid of. It's actually a tour that should be welcomed."
ENGLAND TEAM DIRECTOR ANDY FLOWER

Team director Andy Flower organises an England practice session.

Broad impressed with bat and ball and Kevin Pietersen hinted at a return to form with a first-innings half-century, but it was Strauss who made the most telling contribution as his unbeaten 120 guided the tourists over the line.

"It was satisfying to get a hundred and see the guys home. But I'm sure there are sterner tests ahead," said England's skipper.

"It's always good to get runs early in the tour, but it doesn't count for anything come the first Test match."

Strauss may have been in good touch, but there was concern over the form of fellow opener Alastair Cook, who had struggled for much of the summer and made just 14 runs in his two innings at the WACA.

Things continued to look anything but rosy for Australia, meanwhile, as they were beaten by Sri Lanka in a three-match one-day international series. Defeat in the second game in Sydney represented a seventh successive loss for Ponting's men across all formats, hardly the best preparation for what was about to follow.

"All departments are a little bit wanting at the moment," admitted Australia's captain. "We have to start winning games, it's really important to have that attitude and feeling of winning games around the dressing room and we haven't done that for a while now."

Australia did manage a morale-boosting success in the final match of the series, a dead rubber in Brisbane for which Ponting was rested. Soon after, their forthcoming opponents rolled on to Adelaide to face South Australia and, although the game was disrupted by rain, there were further encouraging signs for England.

Paul Collingwood and Ian Bell struck 94 and 61 respectively in a first-innings total of 288 before a disciplined showing with the ball secured a first-innings lead of 67. Cook then silenced his critics with a composed hundred and Strauss reached three figures for the second successive match as his side coasted to 240 for one declared.

There was not enough time for England to force a positive result, but they remained in buoyant mood, with Strauss particularly delighted by Cook's timely resurgence.

"He batted exceptionally well. It wasn't just the fact he got runs, it was the way he did it," said Strauss of his vice-captain. "His foot movement was very good and his timing was crisp. He'll be feeling pretty good about himself, and that's good for the team."

With the first Test looming ever closer, England opted to rest their frontline bowlers for the final warm-up game against Australia A in Hobart. Anderson, Broad, Finn and Swann were all dispatched to Brisbane, the venue for the Ashes opener, in order to acclimatise, with Chris Tremlett, Tim Bresnan, Ajmal Shahzad and Monty Panesar taking their places in the team.

"The reasoning is that conditions in Hobart are very different to the ones in Brisbane, and we want to give that group of bowlers a little head start," explained Flower.

"They are going three days earlier than the rest of us, and it will also give an opportunity to the other group of bowlers to put their names forward and perform well against Australia A."

On the same day that decision was announced, Australia took the bizarre step of naming a bloated 17-man squad for the series, which provided more questions than answers regarding the potential make-up of their team.

The most talked-about selection was that of Xavier Doherty, an uncapped left-arm spinner with a first-class bowling average of almost 50. Doherty's inclusion, along with that of all-rounder Steven Smith,

"He batted exceptionally well. It wasn't just the fact he got runs, it was the way he did it. He'll be feeling pretty good about himself, and that's good for the team."

ANDREW STRAUSS ON ALASTAIR COOK'S ADELAIDE CENTURY

Alastair Cook's hard work in the nets paid off when he began to find form in the nick of time with a fine hundred in England's second warm-up game, against South Australia at the Adelaide Oval.

increased the pressure on Hauritz, while Hussey and North found their middle-order slots under threat from newcomers Usman Khawaja and Callum Ferguson.

Vice-captain Michael Clarke was expected to shake off a back problem to take his place in the side, while Doug Bollinger and Ryan Harris were both included despite concerns over their fitness.

Smith, Khawaja and Ferguson were given a chance to impress at the Bellerive Oval as Australia A looked to inflict a morale-sapping defeat on England. However, all three failed to make an impression as the tourists surged to a hugely impressive 10-wicket win.

England's back-up bowlers responded well to their call-ups by dismissing their opponents for 230 on day one, with Khawaja and Ferguson making 13 and seven respectively. Bell then took centre stage with a magnificent innings of 192 as England recovered from 137 for five to post a mammoth score of 523.

Smith came in for particular punishment at the hands of the Warwickshire batsman and finished with disappointing figures of two for 118 from 27 largely unthreatening overs. However, the performance of Steven O'Keefe, like Doherty a left-arm spinner, may have attracted the attention of Australia's selectors as he claimed four for 88, including the prized scalp of Pietersen.

O'Keefe had not been included in his country's Ashes squad and the only notable contributions in Australia A's second innings came from two more players who had been left in the cold. Phil Hughes compiled 81 at the top of the order and Cameron White added a defiant 111, but the duo were unable to drag their side back into the game and England took only nine balls to knock off the nine runs they needed for victory.

Australia's second string may have been resoundingly beaten, but the hosts did receive some good news as Hussey proved his worth with a superb hundred for Western Australia in their Sheffield Shield match against Victoria. "I'd be disappointed if I was left out now," admitted Hussey, and it was no surprise to see the veteran left-hander retain his place when Australia's squad was trimmed to 13 players the following day. North also held on to his spot following Khawaja and Ferguson's unimpressive showings in Hobart, but Hauritz was omitted in favour of Doherty, who had impressed in the one-day series against Sri Lanka.

Hauritz may not have set the world on fire during his time as an international cricketer, but he had established himself as a largely reliable performer and many were understandably shocked to see him cast aside in favour of a player totally unproven at Test level.

In an attempt to explain the decision, national selection panel chairman Andrew Hilditch said: "Nathan can consider himself unlucky because his Australian record has been very good over the past 12 months. However, the NSP believes the left-arm orthodox variety Xavier Doherty provides against a predominantly right-handed English middle order is the better option in this game."

Although Hilditch refused to elaborate further, Doherty's selection appeared to be a direct response to Pietersen's apparent weakness against

England batsman Ian Bell hits out on his way to an impressive 192 against Australia A in the warm-up game at the Bellerive Oval in Hobart.

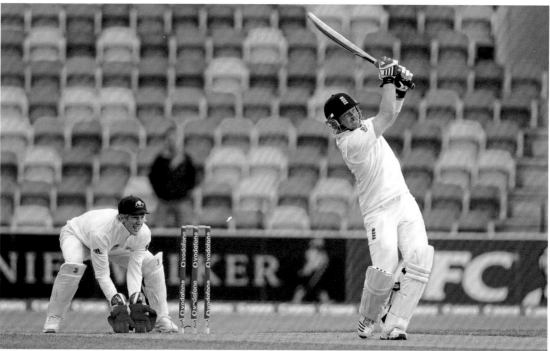

left-arm spin, yet that did little to worry England. "It's not a concern for us, because we've seen Kev destroy left-arm spinners," said Swann. "I know it doesn't worry Kevin – and it doesn't worry the rest of us."

Harris was the other man to be cut from Australia's initial 17-man party as he continued his rehabilitation from a knee injury, while Khawaja briefly returned to the fold as cover for Clarke, whose participation was only confirmed on the eve of the match.

England had no such concerns. Not only were all of their players fit, the majority seemed to be in fine form. Jonathan Trott had been the only member of the top six not to register a score over 50 in the warm-up matches, while the depth of the tourists' bowling resources had been emphasised by events in Hobart.

There could be no doubting which side had enjoyed the smoother build-up to the series and, as the opening day at the Gabba in Brisbane moved ever closer, Strauss remained cautiously optimistic over England's victory chances.

"We're all just very keen to get amongst it now," he said. "I don't think we could be in a much better position than we are at the minute.

"We understand the size of the challenge ahead of us – not many sides come out here and win. But we couldn't be in a better place mentally to take it on.

"It's going to take a lot of good cricket, some guys pulling out some good performances when it really matters, and guys digging pretty deep. But I'm fully confident we have the players able to do that."

At long last, it was time to find out.

"We're all just very keen to get amongst it now. I don't think we could be in a much better position than we are at the minute."
ANDREW STRAUSS

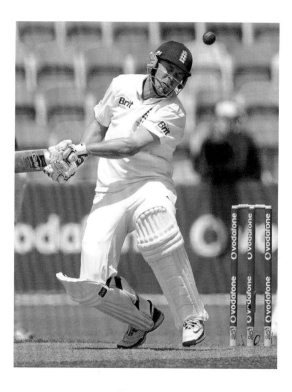

England batsman Jonathan Trott is forced to take avoiding action during his innings against Australia A in Hobart.

First Test Brisbane

25–29 November 2010

After a frenzied build-up spanning several months, England headed into the first Test high on confidence. Securing a first Ashes victory in Australia for 24 years would be a stiff challenge, but preparations could not have gone better and there was a growing belief that this was their time.

2 First Test Brisbane

Alastair Cook emerged as England's leading light in Brisbane following a see-saw opening Test that saw both sides enjoy long periods of dominance. Peter Siddle's hat-trick and a triple-century partnership between Mike Hussey and Brad Haddin looked to have put Australia on course for victory, but by the end of the match it was England who had the momentum, thanks largely to Cook's sensational unbeaten double hundred.

When captain Andrew Strauss departed to the third ball of the first Ashes Test at the Gabba, England's supporters could have been forgiven for thinking, "Here we go again."

The tourists had got off to a similarly dismal start on their previous tour of Australia, when Steve Harmison's opening delivery flew straight to Andrew Flintoff at second slip, and on that occasion they went on to suffer a painful 5-0 whitewash at the hands of a dominant home side.

This time, however, things would be different. By the time that stumps were drawn on the final day in Brisbane, a stunning England rearguard had ensured Strauss's duck no longer appeared significant. Instead, it was his fellow opener, Alastair Cook, who was commanding much of the attention following a heroic display of batsmanship.

Cook contributed a valuable 67 in England's first-innings total of 260, although that effort was overshadowed by the performance of Australia paceman Peter Siddle, who claimed a hat-trick en route to excellent figures of six for 54.

Mike Hussey and Brad Haddin then shared a mammoth partnership of 307 to help Australia to a substantial 221-run lead, but Cook was far from finished. With the assistance of Strauss and Jonathan Trott, who both recorded centuries, the Essex left-hander led his side to safety – and a scarcely believable score of 517 for one declared – with a sensational unbeaten 235. The hosts negotiated the remaining 26 overs without undue alarm, but it was they, rather than England, who would be on the back foot heading into the second Test in Adelaide.

England had gone into the series-opener in positive mood following their impressive form in the warm-up matches. Yet they faced an immediate test of their character on the first morning as Strauss, after

England captain Andrew Strauss is in despair after cutting the third ball of the series to Mike Hussey at gully and departing for a duck.

Jonathan Trott and Alastair Cook continue to pile up the runs for England on the fifth day during their record-breaking partnership.

winning the toss and electing to bat first, carved Ben Hilfenhaus directly to Hussey at gully. Trott survived a number of hairy moments in a skittish innings of 29, which came to an end shortly after drinks when he was bowled through the gate by Shane Watson. But the unflappable Cook stood firm at the other end, sharing partnerships of 76 and 72 with Kevin Pietersen and Ian Bell respectively as England recovered to 197 for four midway through the evening session.

The match appeared evenly poised at that stage, yet there was to be another shift in momentum as Siddle, who had already accounted for Pietersen and Paul Collingwood, marked his 26th birthday with a devastating spell of seam bowling that saw him become only the fourth Australian to claim an Ashes hat-trick.

Cook's 168-ball vigil came to an end as he nibbled at one angled across him and edged to Watson at first slip. England were in even deeper trouble when Matt Prior was bowled via his pads by Siddle's next delivery and Stuart Broad was unable to see off the hat-trick ball, falling lbw to an excellent full-length inswinger which struck him on the boot. Siddle's celebrations – and those of a raucous Gabba crowd – were momentarily halted as Broad opted to review his decision, but there was to be no escape for the tall left-hander. Graeme Swann fell in similar fashion to give Siddle a sixth wicket and England were grateful for the efforts of an in-form Bell, who progressed to 76 with a series of elegant shots before holing out to deep cover off home debutant Xavier Doherty. The innings was brought to an end soon after when Doherty bowled James Anderson and Australia's opening pair of Watson and Simon Katich had few problems in seeing out the day's final seven overs.

England team director Andy Flower was absent from the Gabba on day two as he underwent minor surgery to remove a melanoma on his right cheek, although the Zimbabwean was able to return to his duties later in the Test following the successful operation.

Watson and Katich continued to frustrate England in the morning session as they took their partnership to 78, but the departure of Watson, caught by Strauss at slip off Anderson, triggered another flurry of wickets.

Anderson picked up the key wicket of Ricky Ponting immediately after lunch as the Australia captain was caught down the leg side and Steven Finn then held on to a superb low catch off his own bowling to dismiss Katich. Hussey was fortunate not to fall first ball to Finn as a thick edge fell agonisingly short of Swann at second slip, a moment that was to prove increasingly significant as the innings wore on.

Middlesex youngster Finn did claim a second wicket, however, as Michael Clarke top-edged an attempted pull through to Prior, bringing an end to a torturous innings of nine spanning 50 balls.

Marcus North soon followed for one, Swann picking up a welcome scalp after his first four overs had gone for 34, to leave the hosts reeling on 143 for five. But Hussey and Haddin dug in, adding 77 for the sixth wicket before bad light and rain brought the day to a premature end.

The opening hour of day three provided no shortage of drama as Australia, resuming 40 runs adrift of England's total, looked to move into a position of control. Armed with a new ball, Anderson and Broad performed admirably, but they were unable to gain reward for their efforts.

Hussey was given out leg before to Anderson on one occasion, only for the decision to be overturned on review after replays showed that the ball had pitched marginally outside leg stump, and he was remarkably lucky to survive another huge appeal after the same bowler had struck him plumb in front (England having used up their two referrals by this point). Wicketkeeper-batsman Haddin also struggled early on, particularly at the

"Watching Cook and Trott build that partnership was particularly special. The way we fought back in the game was outstanding. With a 220 deficit, that's a very dangerous situation. I thought the team, and especially those batsmen, showed particularly strong character in fighting their way out of it."

ENGLAND COACH ANDY FLOWER

England celebrate after Andrew Strauss takes a catch at first slip to dismiss Simon Katich off the bowling of Stuart Broad during Australia's second innings.

hands of the accurate Broad, but runs were to prove easier to come by for the batsmen as the day progressed. Hussey, who pulled and drove superbly throughout his innings, brought up his century with a supremely placed drive off Broad wide of mid-off and England were in peril at lunch with the scoreboard reading 329 for five.

The afternoon session failed to bring any relief for the tourists as Australia ruthlessly pressed home their advantage. An increasingly expansive Haddin followed his partner to three figures with a muscular straight six off Swann and a tiring attack appeared to be running out of ideas as runs continued to flow.

The sixth-wicket pair surpassed the previous highest partnership in Tests at Brisbane – 276 between Don Bradman and Lindsay Hassett against New Zealand in 1946 – shortly before tea. But England finally made a breakthrough early in the evening as Haddin pushed at Swann from around the wicket and was caught superbly by Collingwood at slip. Hussey fell three overs later, seven short of a double hundred, when he misjudged a short ball from Finn and picked out Cook at deep midwicket.

Australia crumbled thereafter as Finn ran through the tail to finish with figures of six for 125, but the late wickets did little to detract from the home side's dominance.

Trailing by 221, England faced a daunting task as they set about

Opposing captains Ricky Ponting and Andrew Strauss shake hands at the end of the match after England's second-innings fightback was enough to salvage a draw.

attempting to avoid defeat and their second innings almost got off to the worst possible start when Strauss padded up to Hilfenhaus's first ball and was struck in front of the stumps by a big inswinger. Thankfully for Strauss, umpire Aleem Dar remained unmoved and a review showed he was right to judge that the ball was heading just over the stumps.

England reached the close on 19 without loss before overhauling their deficit in startling fashion on day four. With an increasingly flat pitch offering little assistance to the bowlers, Strauss and Cook were virtually untroubled as they took their opening partnership to 188.

The two left-handers combined diligent defence with accomplished strokeplay throughout their respective innings, although England's captain did receive a let-off on 69 as Mitchell Johnson spilled a relatively straightforward chance at mid-off, Doherty the unfortunate bowler.

Strauss made the most of his reprieve by registering his 19th Test hundred, but he added just 10 further runs before falling victim to North. The part-time off-spinner was arguably Australia's most threatening bowler for much of the fourth day and removed England's skipper with a beautifully flighted delivery that turned sharply past the bat to give Haddin the simplest of stumpings. England were still 33 runs in arrears at the time of Strauss's departure, but Australia were unable to build any pressure as they searched for a second breakthrough, with the erratic Johnson coming in for particular punishment.

Cook cut Siddle through point to bring up his first Ashes century, although he had a scare on 103 as the flame-haired seamer spilled a difficult diving chance at fine leg off Hilfenhaus. There was further frustration for Siddle as Trott picked out a diving Clarke at backward point, only for the ball to squirm out of the fielder's left hand as he landed.

Trott also survived a couple of close lbw shouts, but remained unbeaten on 54 at stumps, with Cook alongside him on 132.

The second-wicket partnership should have been brought to an end

Shane Watson bats out on the final day in an unbroken stand of 92 with skipper Ricky Ponting.

early on the fifth day as a lazy cut shot from Trott picked out Clarke at second slip, but Australia's vice-captain was unable to hold on to the simplest of chances.

England took full advantage thereafter and surpassed a series of records as the game drifted towards a draw. Cook moved to 200 – from 361 balls – with a quick single off Doherty, before Trott brought up his century from the penultimate ball of the morning session, ensuring England's top three batsmen reached three figures in the same innings for only the second time in Tests.

Australia thought they had made the breakthrough when Cook, on 209, appeared to clip one from Doherty to Ponting at short midwicket, but replays failed to conclusively prove whether the ball had carried. Ponting then spilled a tricky chance at slip off Watson to hand Cook another reprieve, but by that stage England had their foot firmly on the accelerator, their aggressive approach typified by a sensational lofted drive from Trott that flew to the boundary.

By the time Strauss called a halt with England on 517 for one, Cook and Trott had overtaken the record partnership in Tests at the Gabba, set earlier in the match by Hussey and Haddin. Cook's total, meanwhile, represented the largest individual score at the ground, beating the previous record of the legendary Bradman.

Australia had little to gain in the brief period of play that remained and when Katich departed to Broad in the sixth over of the innings, caught at slip by Strauss, the most optimistic England fan may even have sensed an unlikely victory.

Watson and Ponting combined to snuff out any such notion with an unbroken partnership of 102, the captain looking in excellent touch as he compiled a 41-ball half-century.

Yet it was England who were to leave Brisbane much the happier side following their stunning fightback.

"The crowd started roaring – it was very loud out there and it definitely did pump me up. I wanted to charge in, bowl fast and try to hit the top of off stump. The execution wasn't quite there, but obviously to hit him (Stuart Broad) on the full like that was a dream ball that I'll remember for a long time."

PETER SIDDLE ON HIS HAT-TRICK BALL

Hat-trick hero

Peter Siddle (above) celebrates with his jubilant Australia team-mates after marking his birthday with a hat-trick on the opening day of the match. He sparked an England collapse by dismissing Alastair Cook (far left) and then bowled Matt Prior (left) before removing Stuart Broad to become only the fourth Australian to claim an Ashes hat-trick.

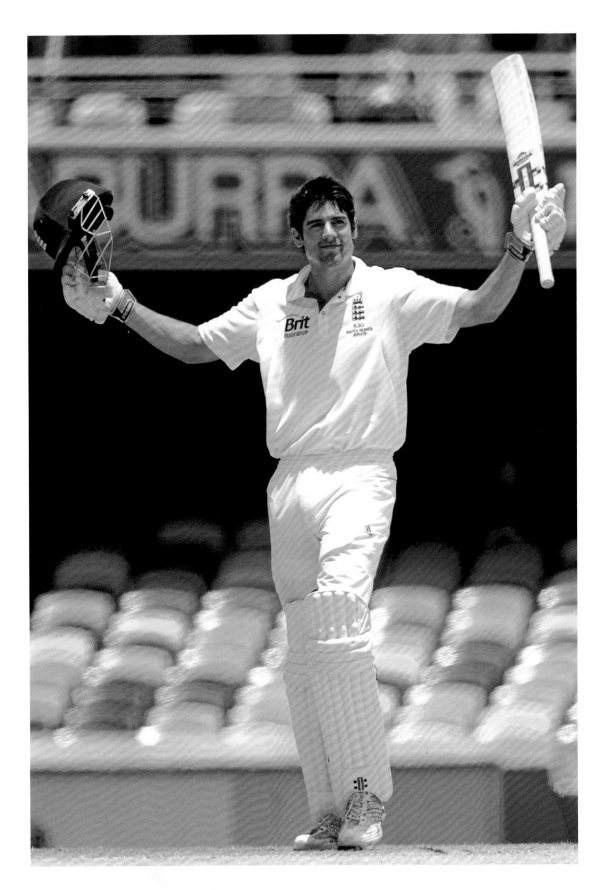

28

"We didn't know about the records, so Trotty and I might have to start digging to see what we have achieved."
ALASTAIR COOK

Ton-up trio
Alastair Cook (left), Jonathan Trott (above) and Andrew Strauss (right) all made centuries during the second innings, only the second time in Test cricket that the top three England batsmen have all reached three figures in an innings.

Mixed fortunes

James Anderson (left) fails to take a difficult chance offered by Brad Haddin, who rode his luck en route to a third Test century. Alastair Cook (above) is more successful as he holds on to dismiss Xavier Doherty, bringing an end to Australia's first innings.

"We've got a lot of belief we can go on and win the series from here. We'll have a spring in our step going to Adelaide."
ANDREW STRAUSS

The first of many
James Anderson jumps for joy after picking up England's first wicket of the series. The Lancashire paceman had Shane Watson caught at first slip by captain Andrew Strauss for 36.

Down and out
A dejected Ricky Ponting
has plenty to ponder as the
tourists pile on the runs
in their second innings.
Australia's bowlers could
only muster one wicket, that
of England captain Andrew
Strauss for 110, despite
toiling away for 152 overs.

FINAL SCORECARD
First Test, Brisbane
25, 26, 27, 28, 29 November 2010
England won the toss and elected to bat

ENGLAND

1ST INNS			R	B	4	6	M
AJ Strauss *	c Hussey	b Hilfenhaus	0	3	0	0	1
AN Cook	c Watson	b Siddle	67	168	6	0	277
IJL Trott		b Watson	29	53	5	0	62
KP Pietersen	c Ponting	b Siddle	43	70	6	0	93
PD Collingwood	c North	b Siddle	4	8	1	0	8
IR Bell	c Watson	b Doherty	76	131	8	0	170
MJ Prior +		b Siddle	0	1	0	0	0
SCJ Broad	lbw	b Siddle	0	1	0	0	0
GP Swann	lbw	b Siddle	10	9	1	0	22
JM Anderson		b Doherty	11	23	2	0	38
ST Finn	not out		0	0	0	0	2
Extras	(b 0, lb 8, w 6, nb 6)		20				
TOTAL			260				

BOWLING

	O	M	R	W
Hilfenhaus	19	4	60	1
Siddle	16	3	54	6
Johnson	15	2	66	0
Watson	12	2	30	1
Doherty	13.5	3	41	2
North	1	0	1	0

2ND INNS			R	B	4	6	M
AJ Strauss *	st Haddin	b North	110	224	15	0	259
AN Cook	not out		235	428	27	0	624
IJL Trott	not out		135	266	19	0	363
Extras	(b 17, lb 4, w 10, nb 6)		37				
TOTAL	(1 wkt dec)		517				

BOWLING

	O	M	R	W
Hilfenhaus	32	8	82	0
Siddle	24	4	90	0
Johnson	27	5	104	0
Watson	15	2	66	0
Doherty	35	5	107	0
North	19	3	47	1

AUSTRALIA

1ST INNS			R	B	4	6	M
SR Watson	c Strauss	b Anderson	36	76	6	0	116
SM Katich	c & b	b Finn	50	106	5	0	165
RT Ponting *	c Prior	b Anderson	10	26	1	0	34
MJ Clarke	c Prior	b Finn	9	50	1	0	81
MEK Hussey	c Cook	b Finn	195	330	26	1	518
MJ North	c Collingwood	b Swann	1	8	0	0	6
BJ Haddin +	c Collingwood	b Swann	136	287	16	1	425
MG Johnson		b Finn	0	19	0	0	33
XJ Doherty	c Cook	b Finn	16	30	2	0	44
PM Siddle	c Swann	b Finn	6	11	1	0	8
BW Hilfenhaus	not out		1	10	0	0	17
Extras	(b 4, lb 12, w 4, nb 1)		21				
TOTAL			481				

BOWLING

	O	M	R	W
Anderson	37	13	99	2
Broad	33	7	72	0
Swann	43	5	128	2
Finn	33.4	1	125	6
Collingwood	12	1	41	0

2ND INNS			R	B	4	6	M
SR Watson	not out		41	97	5	0	101
SM Katich	c Strauss	b Broad	4	16	0	0	24
RT Ponting *	not out		51	43	4	1	76
Extras	(b 4, lb 1, w 1, nb 0)		11				
TOTAL	(1 wkt)		107				

BOWLING

	O	M	R	W
Anderson	5	2	15	0
Broad	7	1	18	1
Swann	8	0	33	0
Finn	4	0	25	0
Pietersen	2	0	6	0

Steven Finn took a six-wicket haul in Australia's first innings.

FALL OF WICKETS

	ENG 1st inns	AUS 1st inns	ENG 2nd inns	AUS 2nd inns
1st	0	78	188	5
2nd	41	96		
3rd	117	100		
4th	125	140		
5th	197	143		
6th	197	450		
7th	197	458		
8th	228	462		
9th	254	472		
10th	260	481		

MATCH DRAWN
Umpires: Aleem Dar and BR Doctrove
* captain + wicketkeeper

MAN OF THE MATCH
Alastair Cook

Batting			R	B	4	6	M
1ST INNINGS	c WATSON	B SIDDLE	67	168	6	0	277
2ND INNINGS	NOT OUT		235*	428	27	0	624
TOTAL			302	596	33	0	901

It is easy to forget that Alastair Cook's place in the England team was said to be under threat heading into the first Ashes Test.

The Essex opener had endured a barren summer with the bat and even a second-innings hundred in the third Test against Pakistan had done little to silence the doubters.

In Brisbane, Cook showed exactly why the selectors had kept faith with him as he took his game to new heights. A gritty 67 proved valuable as England scraped towards a modest total of 260 on day one, but few could have predicted what was in store when the tourists came to bat again, facing a first-innings deficit of 221.

Cook finished unbeaten on 235, the highest score in Tests at the Gabba, and shared

"I was ultra-determined to make it count if I got in again. Luckily I did."
ALASTAIR COOK

mammoth partnerships of 188 and 329 with captain Andrew Strauss and Jonathan Trott respectively (the latter another record) as England racked up 517 for one declared.

By the end of the match, Australia's bowlers appeared at a loss as to how to dismiss the left-hander, a theme that was to continue throughout the series.

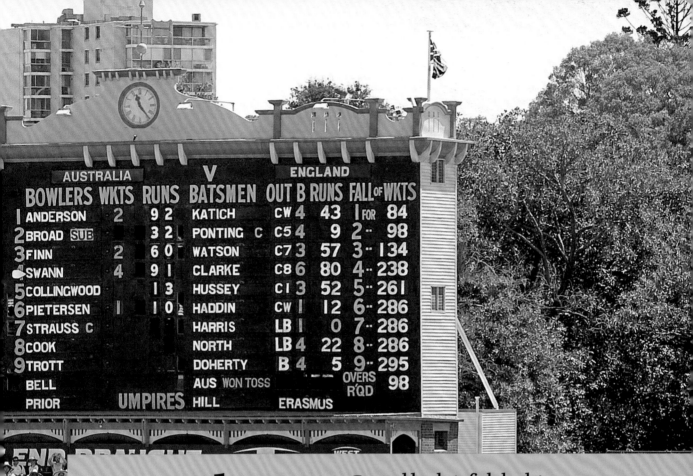

BOWLERS	WKTS	RUNS	BATSMEN	OUT	B	RUNS	FALL OF WKTS	
1 ANDERSON	2	9 2	KATICH	C W	4	43	1 FOR	84
2 BROAD SUB		3 2	PONTING C	C 5	4	9	2 ··	98
3 FINN	2	6 0	WATSON	C 7	3	57	3 ··	134
4 SWANN	4	9 1	CLARKE	C 8	6	80	4 ··	238
5 COLLINGWOOD		1 3	HUSSEY	C 1	3	52	5 ··	261
6 PIETERSEN	1	1 0	HADDIN	C W	1	12	6 ··	286
7 STRAUSS C			HARRIS	LB	1	0	7 ··	286
8 COOK			NORTH	LB	4	22	8 ··	286
9 TROTT			DOHERTY	B	4	5	9 ··	295
BELL			AUS WON TOSS				OVERS R'QD	98
PRIOR		UMPIRES	HILL		ERASMUS			

AUSTRALIA V ENGLAND

Second Test Adelaide

3–7 December 2010

Buoyed by their fightback in Brisbane, England were determined to kick on and secure victory in the second Test. Motivation was never likely to be an issue, particularly as the tourists had a score to settle after suffering a heartbreaking defeat on the same ground four years earlier.

3

Second Test Adelaide

England took a significant step towards Ashes glory with a thoroughly dominant display in Adelaide. James Anderson excelled with the ball on day one as Australia failed to post a competitive total. The tourists' batsmen then made hay once again, Alastair Cook adding another sublime century and Kevin Pietersen registering his highest Test score with a sensational 227. An innings victory was wrapped up on the fifth morning and it was no less than England deserved.

The second Test in Adelaide saw England display their Ashes-winning credentials in the clearest possible fashion as they roared to an emphatic victory by an innings and 71 runs.

The tourists had been able to take plenty of positives from the drawn series-opener at the Gabba, where Australia had been made to toil over the closing two days. In this match, Ricky Ponting's side were on the back foot throughout, unable to recover from a hugely dramatic start that saw them lose their first three wickets for two runs.

England capitalised on their early success by dismissing their opponents for 245, a supreme effort after they had been asked to bowl first on an apparently benign surface. James Anderson was the pick of the attack with four for 51, while a tremendous fielding display resulted in two run-outs and ensured that Australia remained under pressure for the duration of their innings.

A jubilant James Anderson is mobbed by his England team-mates after capturing Ricky Ponting for a golden duck on a dramatic first morning at the Adelaide Oval.

"I was just rushing to get my gear ready really. It was all happening very quickly. I couldn't really believe it, to be honest. Before I blinked, I was out there in the middle."
MIKE HUSSEY ON AUSTRALIA'S EARLY COLLAPSE

38

Jonathan Trott takes the plaudits after running out Simon Katich. The left-handed opener returned to the pavilion without facing a ball and his dismissal set the tone for an abject Australian display.

Alastair Cook then continued where he had left off in Brisbane with another sublime hundred and Kevin Pietersen ended his long wait for a century with a spectacular 227 as England piled on the runs.

They eventually declared on 620 for five, their highest total against Australia since 1938, and although the hosts initially made a better fist of their second innings, they were unable to make England bat again. Graeme Swann picked up five wickets as Australia crumbled to 304 all out on the fifth morning.

England's only concern was an abdominal injury to Stuart Broad, which ruled the seamer out of the remainder of the series.

The first 13 balls of the Test set the tone for what was to follow as Australia suffered a stunning top-order collapse after winning the toss and electing to bat under cloudless skies.

Expectations were for a huge first-innings score at a venue synonymous with 500-plus totals over the first three days, yet England struck with the fourth ball of the match. Anderson appealed loudly for lbw against Shane Watson. That went unanswered but, in the confusion, Watson called Simon Katich through for a single and Jonathan Trott pounced for a direct hit from square leg to run the left-hander out, without facing a ball.

For the second successive match, there had been a dismissal in the opening over and worse was to follow for Australia as skipper Ponting departed for a golden duck. The veteran batsman, playing in his 150th Test, was drawn forward by an outswinging delivery from Anderson and edged low to second slip where Swann took a neat catch away to his left.

England were to enjoy further success from the first ball of Anderson's next over as Michael Clarke, who had already played and missed twice at

39

Broad, attempted another flat-footed drive and provided Swann with a more straightforward chance.

It was Australia's worst start to a Test for 60 years and the hordes of visiting supporters celebrated with a mixture of delirium and shock.

Watson and Mike Hussey were left to pick up the pieces and successfully battled through to lunch, although both men benefited from slices of fortune as the impressive Anderson continued to cause problems. The Lancashire seamer failed to overturn an lbw decision that went in favour of Watson and then dropped a difficult return chance to reprieve Hussey when the Western Australian was on three.

Australia counter-attacked impressively thereafter, both batsmen taking full advantage of anything over-pitched, and Watson brought up his half-century shortly before lunch with a dismissive front-foot pull off Steven Finn.

However, the burly opener was to depart in the second over of the afternoon session as he drove loosely at Anderson and picked out Pietersen at backward point.

Australia's run-rate slowed as Marcus North joined Hussey at the crease. The two left-handers appeared relatively untroubled as they added 60 for the fifth wicket, but their alliance was ended shortly before tea when North, on 26, attempted to cut a delivery from Finn which was too close to him and edged behind.

Hussey continued to accumulate steadily after the interval and moved within sight of a third successive Ashes hundred in the company of Brad Haddin, his fellow centurion in Brisbane. England's bowlers may have been fearing a repeat of the duo's magnificent 307-run stand in the first Test until the previously becalmed Swann struck in the space of successive deliveries.

Hussey had used his feet superbly to combat the off-spinner, but paid the price for a rare lapse in concentration as he stayed back in his crease and edged a drive to Paul Collingwood at slip.

Ryan Harris, who replaced the out-of-form Mitchell Johnson in Australia's bowling line-up, was then trapped lbw first ball and a review proved unsuccessful despite the hot-spot technology suggesting a slight inside edge.

The remaining batsmen provided little resistance, although Haddin did pass 50 before becoming the last man to fall, Finn taking the catch at fine leg after the wicketkeeper had top-edged a hook off Broad.

Strauss and Cook negotiated the single over remaining in the day, yet there was an early setback for England on day two as their captain fell cheaply in the first innings for the second successive match. It appeared Strauss was leaving on the basis of length as he shouldered arms to Doug Bollinger's third delivery, but the decision proved costly as the ball clipped the top of his off-bail. Bollinger had been drafted in to replace

James Anderson enjoys further success with the wicket of Michael Clarke. Australia had slumped to two for three at this stage, their worst start to a Test for 60 years.

> **"It's important to cash in when things do go your way. It's about not getting complacent, it's a mental switch that you have to start at nought again."**
> **ALASTAIR COOK ON HIS LATEST BIG SCORE**

Ben Hilfenhaus in the second change to Australia's line-up and almost picked up a second wicket when Trott, who could have been run out by Xavier Doherty on six, edged to Hussey at gully, only for the fielder to spill a regulation catch.

Trott duly settled in alongside Cook for another substantial partnership, which saw both players grow in confidence as their innings progressed. Cook took Bollinger for three fours in the first over after lunch as England moved serenely past 100.

Australia thought they had removed the opener for 64 when he was given out caught behind attempting to hook Siddle, but the decision was overturned on review as replays showed that the ball had brushed Cook's shoulder.

Trott then had a third "life" as he misjudged a hook shot off Harris and was dropped by Haddin. Harris gained a deserved reward in his next over, however, as Trott failed to get on top of his favourite back-foot punch to midwicket and was well caught by Clarke for 78.

The wicket brought Pietersen to the middle, a player understandably keen to make an impact after spending much of the day – and the best part of two days in Brisbane – padded up waiting to bat.

Doherty came in for particular punishment as England's star batsman displayed his usual level of attacking intent from the outset en route to an attractive 77-ball half-century.

Cook, meanwhile, remained as organised as ever as he moved past 100; the left-hander providing another textbook example of how to construct an innings as he combined sturdy defence and intelligent rotation of the strike with a ruthless ability to punish the bad ball.

By the end of the second day, England were in complete control on 317 for two, with Cook unbeaten on 136 and Pietersen 15 runs short of his first

The look on Ricky Ponting's face says it all as Kevin Pietersen salutes his double hundred. Pietersen cracked 227 from 308 balls in a masterful display of batting.

Test century in 21 months. The landmark arrived early on day three and Pietersen duly moved into top gear as he deposited a dispirited attack to all parts of the ground.

Australia did pick up the wicket of Cook, who was brilliantly caught behind by Haddin for 148 after Harris had found an inside edge. The Gloucester-born batsman had scored 383 runs and batted for 1,058 minutes since his last dismissal, an England record.

Another century stand followed in quick time as Collingwood joined forces with Pietersen, the duo adding 101 in 21 overs before the former was trapped lbw playing back to Watson.

Pietersen subsequently cruised to his second Test double hundred, despite appearing to be inconvenienced by a hamstring problem and, as England pressed on to 551 for four, Australia were no doubt grateful for the rain which ensured there would be no play after tea.

A further 69 runs were added in nine riotous overs on the fourth morning. Pietersen brought up his highest Test score by slog-sweeping the hapless Doherty over midwicket for four, but then edged to Katich at slip attempting to repeat the trick, while Ian Bell and Matt Prior finished unbeaten on 68 and 27 respectively.

With the prospect of rain on the final day, England were determined to make early inroads with the ball once again, but Watson and Katich stood firm in a defiant opening stand of 84.

Katich's innings was particularly impressive given that his mobility had been severely reduced by an Achilles problem that would later require surgery, ruling him out of the remaining three Tests. Yet he was caught behind seven runs short of a half-century after Swann, bowling around the wicket, had got a delivery to turn sharply.

Ponting once again fell cheaply, edging Swann to Collingwood at slip as he played for turn that never came, and although Watson passed 50 for the second time in the match, he was then removed by Finn to leave Australia on 134 for three.

Clarke and Hussey repaired the damage with a century partnership, the former enjoying a long-awaited return to form after a dreadful run of low scores. England looked to have made another breakthrough when the vice-captain was caught at slip off Swann, but Clarke called for a review and replays showed no sign of an inside edge onto pad.

With the penultimate day drawing to a close, Strauss turned to the part-time bowling of Pietersen and was rewarded in stunning fashion. The off-spinner found turn and bounce from his eighth delivery and Clarke, looking to glance off his hips, saw an inside edge ricochet off his thigh pad to Cook at short leg.

England needed to review the decision after umpire Tony Hill, possibly misled by Clarke initially appearing to walk, turned down their appeal, but the correct verdict was reached.

Clarke's dismissal was seen as a key moment and so it proved as Australia crumbled in less than 90 minutes on the final morning.

Hussey received an early let-off when Prior put down a simple chance off Swann, but the in-form batsman failed to make the most of his good fortune and threw his wicket away in tame fashion soon after. An ill-judged pull off Finn provided Anderson with a routine chance at mid-on and he made no mistake to send Hussey packing for 52.

Anderson then took centre stage with the ball, claiming two wickets in as many deliveries. Haddin, driving with minimal foot movement, edged an outswinger through to Prior and Harris bagged a king pair as he shouldered arms to his first delivery and was given lbw.

England had further reason to celebrate two balls later as North was also trapped leg before, England's review proving successful after the batsman had initially survived Swann's lbw shout.

Swann then wrapped up the innings and the match by bowling both Doherty and Siddle and the tourists duly celebrated the most comprehensive of victories.

As predicted, a heavy thunderstorm arrived in the afternoon to leave the ground saturated, but it was too late to save Australia.

Graeme Swann celebrates removing Peter Siddle to end the match.

43

"We're certainly playing well. It's been 18–24 months of solid cricket from us. We're not doing anything special, we're just not doing anything wrong."
GRAEME SWANN

44

Run machine

England batsman Kevin Pietersen in action as he powers his way
to a Test-best score of 227 in the second Test at the Adelaide Oval.

"Individual performances add to a
team victory, and I think the team
victory is incredible. It's the best
feeling, no matter who takes the
wickets or gets the runs."
KEVIN PIETERSEN

46

Painful exit
England seamer Stuart
Broad cannot hide his
disappointment as he sits
alongside bowling coach
David Saker, nursing an
abdominal injury that was to
force him out of the tour.

Hello, goodbye
Ricky Ponting (left) trudges off following his first-ball dismissal at the hands of James Anderson on day one, and the Australia captain is left to reflect on another costly failure with the bat. Brad Haddin (right) has more success, hitting out on his way to a half-century.

"We have got a lot of work to do and we've got some soul-searching to do as individual players."
RICKY PONTING

Hot and cold

Mike Hussey compiled a
defiant 93 on day one (above),
but threw his wicket away in
Australia's second innings as a
miscued pull off Steven Finn
provided James Anderson with
a simple catch (left).

Error of judgement

Andrew Strauss (right)
immediately regrets his
decision to offer no shot as he
is bowled by Doug Bollinger's
third delivery on day two. It
was to be a rare moment of
success for the home attack.

"We never gave them a look-in,
and we're very pleased about what
we've done. But we know the
game of cricket, and we know it's
got a horrible way of biting you
if you pat yourself on the back
too much."

ANDREW STRAUSS

49

Stormy weather
Dark clouds threaten to wreck England's victory push on day four. The ground was eventually saturated by heavy rain on the following afternoon, but by then the tourists had wrapped up a comprehensive innings win.

FINAL SCORECARD
Second Test, Adelaide
3, 4, 5, 6, 7 December 2010
Australia won the toss and elected to bat

AUSTRALIA

1ST INNS			R	B	4	6	M
SR Watson	c Pietersen	b Anderson	51	94	7	1	129
SM Katich	run out (Trott)		0	0	0	0	3
RT Ponting *	c Swann	b Anderson	0	1	0	0	0
MJ Clarke	c Swann	b Anderson	2	6	0	0	6
MEK Hussey	c Collingwood	b Swann	93	183	8	0	296
MJ North	c Prior	b Finn	26	93	4	0	99
BJ Haddin + ...	c Finn	b Broad	56	95	3	1	145
RJ Harris	lbw	b Swann	0	1	0	0	0
XJ Doherty	run out (Strauss)		6	19	1	0	26
PM Siddle	c Cook	b Anderson	3	21	0	0	23
DE Bollinger	not out		0	3	0	0	7
Extras	(b 0, lb 6, w 1, nb 1)		8				
TOTAL			245				

BOWLING

	O	M	R	W
Anderson	19	4	51	4
Broad	18.5	6	39	1
Finn........................	16	1	71	1
Swann.....................	29	2	70	2
Collingwood	3	0	8	0

2ND INNS			R	B	4	6	M
SR Watson	c Strauss	b Finn	57	141	10	0	180
SM Katich...............	c Prior	b Swann	43	85	6	0	112
RT Ponting *	c Collingwood	b Swann	9	19	2	0	21
MJ Clarke...............	c Cook	b Pietersen	80	139	11	0	231
MEK Hussey...........	c Anderson	b Finn	52	107	5	1	208
MJ North	lbw	b Swann	22	35	3	0	56
BJ Haddin + ...	c Prior	b Anderson	12	21	2	0	24
RJ Harris................	lbw	b Anderson	0	1	0	0	0
XJ Doherty...............		b Swann	5	9	1	0	17
PM Siddle................		b Swann	6	22	1	0	29
DE Bollinger	not out		7	16	1	0	14
Extras	(b 5, lb 1, w 5, nb 0)		11				
TOTAL			304				

BOWLING

	O	M	R	W
Anderson	22	4	92	2
Broad	11	3	32	0
Finn........................	18	2	60	2
Swann.....................	41.1	12	91	5
Collingwood	4	0	13	0
Pietersen	3	0	10	1

ENGLAND

1ST INNS			R	B	4	6	M
AJ Strauss *		b Bollinger	1	3	0	0	1
AN Cook	c Haddin	b Harris	148	269	18	0	422
IJL Trott	c Clarke	b Harris	78	144	12	0	212
KP Pietersen	c Katich	b Doherty	227	308	34	1	548
PD Collingwood	lbw	b Watson	42	70	6	0	97
IR Bell	not out		68	97	8	1	267
MJ Prior + ...	not out		27	21	2	0	24
SCJ Broad							
GP Swann							
JM Anderson							
ST Finn							
Extras	(b 8, lb 13, w 8, nb 0)		29				
TOTAL	(5 wkts dec)		620				

BOWLING

	O	M	R	W
Harris.......................	29	5	84	2
Bollinger...................	29	1	130	1
Siddle......................	30	3	121	0
Watson.....................	19	7	44	1
Doherty	27	3	158	1
North	18	0	62	0

Graeme Swann celebrates dismissing Xavier Doherty, one of his five wickets in Australia's second innings.

FALL OF WICKETS

	AUS 1st inns	ENG 1st inns	AUS 2nd inns
1st	0	3	84
2nd	0	176	98
3rd	2	351	134
4th............................	96	452	238
5th............................	156	568	261
6th............................	207		286
7th............................	207		286
8th............................	226		286
9th............................	243		295
10th..........................	245		304

ENGLAND WON BY AN INNINGS AND 71 RUNS
Umpires: M Erasmus and AL Hill
* captain + wicketkeeper

MAN OF THE MATCH
Kevin Pietersen

Batting			R	B	4	6	M
1st Inns			227	308	34	1	548
Bowling			O	M	R	W	
2nd Inns			3	0	10	1	

There was plenty for England to smile about after the second Ashes Test, not least the long-awaited return to form of Kevin Pietersen.

The South Africa-born batsman put Australia to the sword with a swashbuckling 227 in Adelaide, ending a 21-month barren run in which he had failed to reach three figures in a Test match.

Pietersen may be renowned for his self-confidence, but he had clearly been affected by his loss of form and his relief was clear to see as he brought up his 17th Test hundred on the third morning of the match.

From then on we were treated to the Pietersen of old as he collected boundaries almost at will. England's number four raced from 100 to 150 in only 52 balls before knuckling down again and

> "I wouldn't say it's the Ashes in particular. But I do love the big occasion; I do love challenging myself against the best players in the world."
>
> KEVIN PIETERSEN

surpassing his previous highest Test score of 226, which he achieved against the West Indies in May 2007.

As if that was not enough, Pietersen then picked up the key wicket of Michael Clarke late on day four with his part-time off-spin, a crucial blow as England marched towards a spectacular innings victory.

53

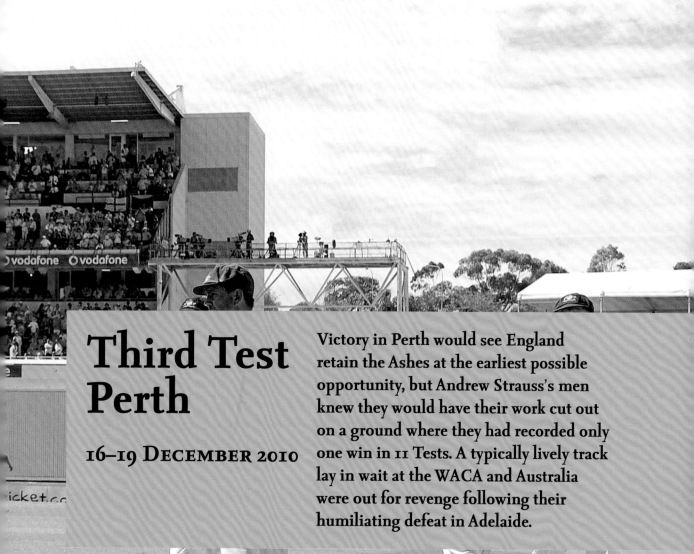

Third Test
Perth

16–19 December 2010

Victory in Perth would see England
retain the Ashes at the earliest possible
opportunity, but Andrew Strauss's men
knew they would have their work cut out
on a ground where they had recorded only
one win in 11 Tests. A typically lively track
lay in wait at the WACA and Australia
were out for revenge following their
humiliating defeat in Adelaide.

4 Third Test Perth

Mitchell Johnson enjoyed a sensational return to form as Australia bounced back from another woeful start to claim a convincing series-levelling victory. The recalled left-arm paceman contributed vital runs with the bat before hitting top form with the ball on a Perth pitch offering plenty of assistance to the seamers. Chris Tremlett impressed on his return to the England side with eight wickets, but his efforts were overshadowed by Johnson and Ryan Harris, who claimed nine wickets each.

At the end of the opening day in Perth it was difficult to envisage a way back for Australia. For the second successive match, Ricky Ponting's side had been dismissed for a seemingly below-par total in their first innings, although their score of 268 actually represented a recovery of sorts after they had slumped to 69 for five shortly after lunch.

A buoyant England reached stumps on 29 without loss and appeared set to march towards the victory that would have seen them retain the Ashes with two games to spare. But there was to be a dramatic twist in the tale as Australia, inspired by a rejuvenated Mitchell Johnson, launched a spectacular fightback to secure a comprehensive 267-run win.

Johnson had been pilloried following his dismal display in the first Test at the Gabba, which resulted in him being dropped for the following match in Adelaide. However, after striking 62 with the bat on day one, the recalled left-arm paceman took centre stage at the WACA with a stunning display of swing bowling that yielded outstanding figures of six for 38.

England were dismissed for 187 and soon found themselves in deeper trouble as Mike Hussey and Shane Watson contributed 116 and 95

> "I'm frustrated, no doubt about it, not to get a hundred. Of course I'd definitely take 90 any time I go out to bat but I'm disappointed I couldn't go on with it."
> **Shane Watson**

Mike Hussey punishes a short ball on his way to a century during the second innings which helped to give Australia a commanding lead.

respectively to lift the hosts to 309 in their second innings. Chris Tremlett, playing in place of Stuart Broad, claimed an impressive five-wicket haul, taking his tally for the match to eight, but his efforts were to prove in vain as England suffered a second batting collapse. They were bundled out for 123 on the fourth morning, with Ryan Harris taking six for 47 and man of the match Johnson picking up a further three wickets.

The result left the series tantalisingly poised at 1-1 heading into the Boxing Day Test in Melbourne and the tourists, so dominant in Adelaide, suddenly had plenty to ponder.

England had got off to another excellent start after Andrew Strauss won the toss and opted to bowl first on a green pitch. For the first time in the series, there was to be no wicket in the opening over of the match, but Phil Hughes didn't last much longer. The diminutive left-hander, who replaced the injured Simon Katich in one of four changes to Australia's line-up, was bowled as he played across the line to Tremlett's sixth delivery.

Ponting, a man under increasing pressure due to his personal form and the performances of his team, collected three early boundaries, but he too departed to a rash stroke, chasing a wide delivery from James Anderson that he could easily have left alone. That said, it took a remarkable catch to complete the dismissal as Paul Collingwood dived high to his right to pluck the ball out of the air one-handed.

Michael Clarke was another batsman to give his wicket away in injudicious fashion. He made only four before fencing at a back-of-a-length ball from Tremlett and providing Matt Prior with a routine catch.

England soon made another breakthrough as Watson, who had successfully referred a caught-behind decision in the first over and was also dropped by Strauss on two, was trapped lbw by a Steven Finn yorker. The batsman once again turned to the review system in a bid to overturn the verdict, but replays showed that the ball had struck boot before bat.

Australia's decision to bat leg-spinning all-rounder Steven Smith at six surprised many and the youngster never looked settled during his 37-ball stay at the crease, which ended shortly after lunch when he played away from his body to Tremlett and edged to Strauss at first slip.

Familiar scenes ensued as Hussey and Brad Haddin joined forces in a defiant partnership of 68. However, on this occasion, Hussey was unable to kick on and he fell for 61 when a faint edge off Swann was taken by Prior, England requiring a review to confirm the decision.

Haddin also recorded a half-century, but when he and Harris fell in quick succession after tea, Australia were in disarray and only some spirited lower-order batting lifted them past 250. Johnson led the way, striking eight fours and a six in an entertaining knock, while Peter Siddle and Ben Hilfenhaus also contributed valuable runs as the ninth and 10th-wicket stands added a combined total of 67.

England's frustration gradually diminished as Strauss and Alastair Cook saw off the new ball before taking their partnership to 78 on the second morning. But they would be left to rue their failure to finish off Australia's innings as Johnson turned the match on its head, claiming three wickets in 12 balls either side of the drinks interval.

Cook was denied the opportunity to register another mammoth score when, on 32, he sliced a drive to Hussey at gully, and both Jonathan Trott and Kevin Pietersen were lbw to deliveries that swung late. The triple strike sparked new life into the hosts and Harris added to their jubilation with the key dismissal of Strauss, caught behind for 52.

Johnson then picked up a fourth scalp as another wonderful inswinger beat Collingwood for pace and thundered into the Durham batsman's pads. Collingwood was initially spared by umpire Marais Erasmus, only for a review to show that the ball would have gone on to hit the stumps.

Out of nowhere, England found themselves 98 for five and they continued to struggle after lunch as Australia's four-pronged seam attack extracted plenty of movement from a lively surface. A valuable stand of 47

"I've worked hard to get back to where I want to be. If you want something bad enough you work out how to do it."
CHRIS TREMLETT

Double trouble as Kevin Pietersen and Paul Collingwood trudge off towards the dressing room after they were both dismissed lbw by Mitchell Johnson on the second morning.

between Ian Bell and Prior came to an end as the keeper was bowled, via hip and glove, by Siddle, who gained his reward following a fierce barrage of short deliveries.

Graeme Swann also provided useful support to Bell, but their hard work was undone as the final four wickets fell for the addition of just six runs. Swann was caught behind off Harris and although Bell brought up a third consecutive 50, he fell to the same bowler when a loose drive flew to Ponting at second slip. Johnson then returned to dismiss Tremlett and Anderson, giving his team a healthy first-innings lead of 81.

England knew early wickets were essential if they were to stay in the game and their bowlers enjoyed further success against Australia's top order as a fascinating match continued to ebb and flow.

Hughes avoided the ignominy of another single-figure score but managed only 12 before being caught at third slip by Collingwood off Finn, who then had Ponting caught down the leg side for one.

The tourists did not have to wait long for another scalp as Clarke, after racing to 20 unconvincingly, played on to Tremlett. Clarke's departure left Australia 61 for three and the match looked to be in the balance once more, but Watson and Hussey refused to panic and led their team into a position of dominance with a 113-run partnership for the fourth wicket.

A first Ashes century eluded Watson yet again as he fell lbw to Tremlett for 95 on the third morning. The value of his contribution, however, could not be overestimated.

Hussey continued to make hay following the opener's departure and became the first player to score six successive half-centuries in Ashes

contests, although he and Smith each had to successfully review decisions
that had initially gone against them during a fifth-wicket stand of 75.

Smith's luck ran out on 36 as he gloved a short ball from Tremlett
through to Prior and Haddin, who got off the mark by sweeping Swann
for six, followed soon after to give the Surrey paceman a fourth scalp.

Wickets continued to fall at regular intervals as England rallied either
side of tea, with Hussey the last man to fall for a marvellous 116. The left-
hander had been under severe pressure heading into the first Test, but by
the end of this innings he had scored a sensational 517 runs in the series.

Tremlett picked up the wicket of the centurion to finish with five for 87,
but his side would need to chase down a daunting total of 391 if they were
to emerge victorious and, in truth, they never threatened to do so.

The early exit of Cook, who had earlier been overtaken by Hussey as the
leading run-scorer in the series, was a significant blow. England's vice-
captain made 13 before being trapped lbw as he played back to a Harris
delivery that nipped back off the seam.

Johnson got back in on the act with the dismissal of Strauss, caught
by his opposite number Ponting following a leaden-footed drive, and
Pietersen also departed cheaply as he nicked Hilfenhaus to Watson at first
slip. Trott and Collingwood looked set to bat out the remainder of day
three, but Australia were not finished and claimed wickets in the final two

60

overs to put the result of the match almost beyond doubt. It was Johnson who once again provided the inspiration as he ousted Trott with his penultimate delivery. A thick edge was parried by Ponting at second slip, but wicketkeeper Haddin had little trouble in collecting the rebound.

Ponting was forced to leave the field after injuring the little finger on his left hand as he dropped the initial chance, but his team were able to celebrate another breakthrough from the last ball of the day as Collingwood, playing away from his body in similar fashion to Trott, edged Harris to Smith at third slip.

Australia's players were understandably jubilant and wasted little time in completing their task the following morning, in the continued absence of Ponting. Harris bagged four of the five wickets required, starting with the removal of nightwatchman Anderson, who was bowled by one that appeared to keep a shade low.

When Bell was trapped lbw by the same bowler, any hope of a miraculous England fightback had disappeared and the tail offered little resistance. Harris saw off Prior to secure a maiden five-wicket haul and, after Johnson had bowled Swann, captured Finn to bring an end to the match. With two Tests still to come, the teams were back on level terms and, given the frequent swings in momentum thus far, it was impossible to predict what would happen next.

"**We have to retain a sense of perspective. This result doesn't make us a bad team overnight. We need to retain the confidence we built from the first two Tests and come out all guns blazing in Melbourne. Now is not a time for panic.**"
ANDREW STRAUSS

Double delight as Ryan Harris claims the wickets of Ian Bell (left) and Alastair Cook (right) on his way to a maiden five-wicket haul in Test cricket.

62

Zero to hero
Mitchell Johnson made the
most of his recall, making 62 in
Australia's first innings (above)
before dismissing Andrew
Strauss (left) early in England's
second innings on his way to a
nine-wicket match haul.

"Credit to Mitchell Johnson and
Australia – they came back hard,
which we knew they would at
some point in this series."
IAN BELL

63

Bowled over

The seagulls seem unimpressed after Australia vice-captain Michael Clarke (left) has his middle stump knocked back by Chris Tremlett during the second innings.

Close call

Steven Smith (below left) is forced into a despairing dive as he scrambles to make his ground under pressure from an England fielder.

Jump for joy

Mike Hussey (right) leaps into the air with delight as he celebrates reaching three figures to put Australia firmly in control of the match.

65

"We've had plenty of doubters and we knew we had to turn things around quick. It's great for the boys to play the way they did."
RICKY PONTING

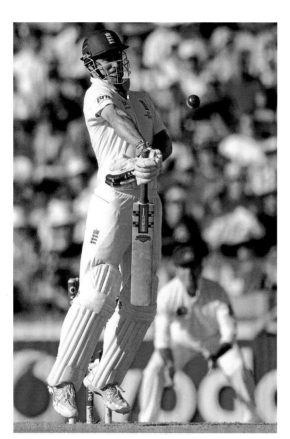

Into the light
Australia seamer Ryan Harris (right), who ended the match with nine wickets, sends down another delivery in the late afternoon sun.

On his toes
England captain Andrew Strauss (left) tries to deal with a short ball as his side battle to stay in the game on a lively wicket in Perth.

Making a point
Matt Prior (below left) has a frank exchange of words with Peter Siddle as he leaves the pitch having been bowled by the paceman.

Thumbs up
Australia captain Ricky Ponting (above) has something to celebrate about at last after his side levelled the series and (left) talks to spin legend Shane Warne during the post-match presentations.

"That spell from Mitchell Johnson on the second morning ripped apart our top order. We were always behind after that and credit to them for not letting us back in."
ANDREW STRAUSS

Food for thought
England captain Andrew Strauss (above right) and pace duo Chris Tremlett and James Anderson (right) have plenty to ponder as the tourists suffer their first defeat of the tour.

FINAL SCORECARD
Third Test, Perth
16, 17, 18, 19 December 2010
England won the toss and elected to bowl

AUSTRALIA

1ST INNS			R	B	4	6	M
SR Watson .... lbw		b Finn	13	40	1	0	78
PJ Hughes		b Tremlett	2	6	0	0	10
RT Ponting * .... c Collingwood	b Anderson		12	10	3	0	12
MJ Clarke .... c Prior	b Tremlett		4	10	1	0	13
MEK Hussey .... c Prior	b Swann		61	104	9	1	148
SPD Smith .... c Strauss	b Tremlett		7	37	0	0	47
BJ Haddin + ... c Swann	b Anderson		53	80	6	1	123
MG Johnson .... c Anderson	b Finn		62	93	8	1	121
RJ Harris	b Anderson		3	5	0	0	8
PM Siddle .... not out			35	59	3	0	72
BW Hilfenhaus .... c Cook	b Swann		13	12	3	0	22
Extras	(b 0, lb 3, w 0, nb 0)		3				
TOTAL			268				

BOWLING

	O	M	R	W
Anderson	20	3	61	3
Tremlett	23	3	63	3
Finn...........................	15	1	86	2
Collingwood	2	0	3	0
Swann.......................	16	0	52	2

2ND INNS			R	B	4	6	M
SR Watson .... lbw		b Tremlett	95	174	11	0	239
PJ Hughes .... c Collingwood	b Finn		12	31	1	0	55
RT Ponting * .... c Prior	b Finn		1	9	0	0	19
MJ Clarke	b Tremlett		20	18	4	0	20
MEK Hussey .... c Swann	b Tremlett		116	172	15	0	314
SPD Smith .... c Prior	b Tremlett		36	62	2	0	84
BJ Haddin + ...	b Tremlett		7	10	0	1	21
MG Johnson .... c Bell	b Collingwood		1	4	0	0	4
RJ Harris .... c Bell	b Finn		1	7	0	0	13
PM Siddle .... c Collingwood	b Anderson		8	26	1	0	32
BW Hilfenhaus .... not out			0	5	0	0	7
Extras	(b 0, lb 6, w 4, nb 2)		12				
TOTAL			309				

BOWLING

	O	M	R	W
Anderson	26	7	65	1
Tremlett	24	4	87	5
Finn...........................	21	4	97	3
Collingwood	6	3	3	1
Swann.......................	9	0	51	0

ENGLAND

1ST INNS			R	B	4	6	M
AJ Strauss * .... c Haddin	b Harris		52	102	8	0	129
AN Cook .... c Hussey	b Johnson		32	63	3	1	91
IJL Trott .... lbw	b Johnson		4	8	1	0	10
KP Pietersen .... lbw	b Johnson		0	3	0	0	1
PD Collingwood ...... lbw	b Johnson		5	17	0	0	25
IR Bell .... c Ponting	b Harris		53	90	6	0	136
MJ Prior + ...	b Siddle		12	42	1	0	64
GP Swann .... c Haddin	b Harris		11	31	1	0	48
CT Tremlett	b Johnson		2	14	0	0	20
JM Anderson .... c Watson	b Johnson		0	6	0	0	6
ST Finn .... not out			1	1	0	0	1
Extras	(b 8, lb 4, w 1, nb 2)		15				
TOTAL			187				

BOWLING

	O	M	R	W
Hilfenhaus..................	21	6	53	0
Harris.........................	15	4	59	3
Siddle.........................	9	2	25	1
Johnson	17.3	5	38	6

2ND INNS			R	B	4	6	M
AJ Strauss * .... c Ponting	b Johnson		15	35	3	0	39
AN Cook .... lbw	b Harris		13	16	1	0	23
IJL Trott .... c Haddin	b Johnson		31	61	3	0	90
KP Pietersen .... c Watson	b Hilfenhaus		3	23	0	0	40
PD Collingwood ...... c Smith	b Harris		11	27	1	0	39
JM Anderson	b Harris		3	14	0	0	20
IR Bell .... lbw	b Harris		16	23	3	0	33
MJ Prior + ... c Hussey	b Harris		10	9	0	1	18
GP Swann	b Johnson		9	5	1	0	8
CT Tremlett .... not out			1	3	0	0	11
ST Finn .... c Smith	b Harris		2	7	0	0	6
Extras	(b 0, lb 8, w 0, nb 1)		9				
TOTAL			123				

BOWLING

	O	M	R	W
Hilfenhaus..................	10	4	16	1
Harris.........................	11	1	47	6
Siddle.........................	4	1	8	0
Johnson	12	3	44	3

Chris Tremlett's eight wickets in the match proved in vain.

FALL OF WICKETS

	AUS 1st inns	ENG 1st inns	AUS 2nd inns	ENG 2nd inns
1st	2	78	31	23
2nd.....................	17	82	34	37
3rd......................	28	82	64	55
4th......................	36	94	177	81
5th......................	69	98	252	81
6th......................	137	145	271	94
7th......................	189	181	276	111
8th......................	201	186	284	114
9th......................	233	186	308	120
10th.....................	268	187	309	123

AUSTRALIA WON BY 267 RUNS
Umpires: BR Doctrove and M Erasmus
* captain + wicketkeeper

MAN OF THE MATCH
Mitchell Johnson

Batting				R	B	4	6	M
1st Inns				62	93	8	1	121
2nd Inns				1	4	0	0	4
TOTAL				63	97	8	1	125
Bowling				O	M	R	W	
1st Inns				17.3	5	38	6	
2nd Inns				12	3	44	3	
TOTAL				19.3	8	82	9	

Awful in the first Test and unceremoniously dropped for the second, Mitchell Johnson delivered a sensational reminder of his talent at the WACA.

Buoyed by a counter-attacking 62 in Australia's first innings, the left-arm paceman tore through England's line-up with a devastating display of swing bowling on day two.

In returning outstanding figures of six for 38 from 17.3 overs, Johnson not only wrecked the tourists' hopes of a first-innings lead but also breathed new life into an Australia side desperately short of confidence following seven consecutive days of English domination.

The lively surface in Perth was a key factor in Johnson's revival, but his performance was still a major surprise after he had posed so little threat in the series-opener at the Gabba.

Ricky Ponting's side never looked back and their eventual victory was every bit as comprehensive as England's in Adelaide. Johnson added three further wickets to his tally in the second innings and, although fellow seamer Ryan Harris also finished with nine victims in the match, there was no doubting who had made the more significant impact on the match.

> "I was disappointed to miss out in Adelaide. You don't want to miss a Test for your country but it has worked in my favour. I got to work on a few things and get the confidence back."
> **MITCHELL JOHNSON**

71

Fourth Test Melbourne

26–29 December 2010

There was a feverish sense of excitement ahead of the Boxing Day Test at the MCG. Australia had brought the series back to life with victory in Perth and home fans had high hopes of a repeat. England, however, remained one win away from retaining the Ashes. The stakes could not have been higher.

5

Fourth Test Melbourne

England secured the Ashes after reasserting their hold over Australia in stunning fashion at the MCG. Ricky Ponting's men were bundled out for 98 on day one and never recovered as Jonathan Trott's unbeaten century helped England to a mammoth first-innings lead. The tourists duly sailed to their second innings victory of the series, ensuring they would keep the famous little urn regardless of the outcome in the final Test in Sydney.

The 2010 Boxing Day Test will live long in the memory of England cricket fans. Not only did their team finally retain the Ashes in Australia, for the first time in 24 years, they did so in the most comprehensive manner, winning the fourth Test by an innings and 157 runs.

England's victory was set up by a stunning opening-day performance, which saw them dismiss the hosts for a paltry 98 before reaching the close on 157 without loss. James Anderson and Chris Tremlett were the chief destroyers with the ball as they collected four wickets apiece, while Tim Bresnan justified his call-up at the expense of Steven Finn with commendable figures of two for 25 from 13 overs.

Andrew Strauss's side went on to post 513, thanks largely to Jonathan Trott's wonderful unbeaten 168, and a demoralised Australia were unable to respond in their second innings as they crumbled to 258 all out. Bresnan returned four for 50 to cap a marvellous Ashes debut and it was he who claimed the prized final wicket as Ben Hilfenhaus edged through to Matt Prior.

Wild celebrations ensued as England's players basked in the glory of a truly memorable achievement. Their mission was far from complete, with Australia still able to level the series in the final match at the SCG, but the primary objective had been attained.

By contrast, it was a time of sober reflection for Ricky Ponting, who had become the first Australia captain since the 19th century to lose the Ashes three times. The Tasmanian shrugged off a broken finger to feature in the fourth Test, but once again came in for heavy criticism from the media. His frustration was evident on the second day as he engaged in an unsavoury spat with the umpires after a referral had gone in Kevin Pietersen's favour. Ponting later apologised for his actions, which resulted

Chris Tremlett celebrates another cheap dismissal of Ricky Ponting as the Australia captain's poor form with the bat continues.

75

James Anderson looks back to the umpire for confirmation that he has claimed the prized wicket of Mike Hussey, who was caught behind for a duck during the first innings.

in him losing 40 per cent of his match fee, but it remained to be seen whether he would lead Australia in Sydney.

England's bowlers had got their team off to a fine start in the previous two Tests, but managed to surpass their efforts in Adelaide and Perth with a marvellous collective display after Strauss had elected to field first for the second successive game.

A crowd of more than 84,000 watched in shock and disbelief as Australia capitulated either side of lunch, their lack of discipline reflected in the fact that all 10 batsmen departed to catches behind the wicket, with Prior alone claiming six victims.

There was initial frustration for Anderson, who had Shane Watson put down in each of his first two overs. Paul Collingwood spilled a difficult chance low to his left at third slip, while Pietersen put down a more straightforward opportunity at gully.

Watson failed to take advantage, however, and it was not long before he gloved a lifting delivery from Tremlett to provide Pietersen with the simplest chance to redeem himself.

Phil Hughes raised further question marks over his suitability as a Test match opener with another ill-judged stroke, Pietersen taking another catch at gully after the left-hander had attempted to thrash Bresnan through the covers on the up.

Australia then lost a third wicket without adding to their score as Tremlett got another delivery to rise sharply and the ball flew off the splice of Ponting's bat to Graeme Swann at second slip. England were buoyant, but it was the dismissal of the in-form Mike Hussey, caught behind in the final over before lunch, that brought them the greatest joy.

Anderson was the man to make that key breakthrough and he gained further rewards after the interval as Australia lost their last six wickets for the addition of 40 runs. Steven Smith and Michael Clarke both failed to deal with lateral movement as they nicked to Prior and, after Brad Haddin had edged a wild drive off Bresnan to Strauss at first slip, Mitchell Johnson duly followed.

The scoreboard read 77 for eight at that stage and when Tremlett returned to dismiss Peter Siddle and Ben Hilfenhaus, Australia had slumped to their lowest completed first-innings total in a home Ashes Test since 1888.

With memories of Australia's fightback in Perth still fresh in their minds, England's openers set about their task with steely determination. Alastair Cook had a scare on 27 when Hilfenhaus successfully appealed for lbw, but the decision was overturned after replays revealed an inside edge onto his pad and the batsmen were relatively untroubled for the rest of the day as Australia's seam attack, so potent in Perth, failed to build any pressure. England had comfortably surpassed Australia's score by the time stumps were drawn, with Cook unbeaten on 80 and Strauss on 64.

The duo added only seven runs between them on day two before each fell victim to a fired-up Siddle. Cook was caught low down at first slip by Watson, before Strauss saw a leading edge superbly taken by Hussey at backward point.

Trott steadied the ship and added 92 with Pietersen either side of lunch to reassert England's dominance. Pietersen was fortunate to see an edge land short of second slip early on as Siddle continued to impress, but he soon settled into his stride and appeared on course to record another huge score as he took the attack to Smith shortly before lunch.

The new ball eventually accounted for Pietersen in the afternoon session, but only after England's number four had been involved in a controversial incident that saw Ponting lose his cool. Pietersen was one short of his half-century when Haddin convinced his team-mates to review Aleem Dar's not-out decision off the bowling of Ryan Harris. No

"I accept the discussion went on for too long and I understand the reasons for the dissent charge handed down by the ICC. However, I would be unhappy if anyone thought I was being disrespectful towards the umpires as this wasn't my intention."
RICKY PONTING

Ricky Ponting takes his frustration out on umpire Aleem Dar after a referral failed to back up Australia's belief that Kevin Pietersen had edged behind to Brad Haddin.

evidence emerged to support Australia's review, and the initial verdict was duly confirmed. But Ponting reacted furiously and, along with Siddle, berated Dar, and then his colleague Tony Hill, in an unseemly incident that halted play for minutes rather than seconds.

Pietersen was unable to add to Australia's misery and fell soon after for 51, lbw to a Siddle delivery that jagged back off the seam. Collingwood and Ian Bell then departed in similar fashion as they each pulled Johnson to Siddle at fine leg.

Although his bowling remained erratic, Johnson almost claimed a third scalp before tea as Prior feathered an edge through to Haddin. However, England's wicketkeeper survived after umpire Dar called for a replay, which showed the seamer had overstepped. Prior made the most of his reprieve and both he and Trott scored freely for the remainder of the day to kill off any hopes of another Australian comeback.

Trott required treatment from the physio after playing a Ben Hilfenhaus delivery onto his own knee but shrugged off the setback to bring up his hundred with a trademark clip through midwicket off Harris. By the end of the day, the sixth-wicket partnership was worth 158, and Prior was within sight of his own century.

The Sussex man was unable to reach that landmark on the third morning and fell for 85 when he clipped Siddle to Ponting at mid-on.

The celebrations begin for England as Tim Bresnan has Ben Hilfenhaus caught behind by Matt Prior to complete an Ashes-retaining victory at the MCG.

Jonathan Trott raises his bat as he completes a run to deservedly take him into three figures.

Siddle soon picked up a deserved fifth wicket as he had Bresnan caught behind for four, but the rest of Australia's attack was in disarray. Harris would play no further part in the match after pulling up lame with a stress fracture of his left ankle, Hilfenhaus continued to look a shadow of the bowler who toured England 18 months earlier and an increasingly wayward Johnson conceded 31 runs in a poor four-over spell.

Swann handed out the bulk of the punishment to Johnson in an entertaining cameo, which ended on 22 when he edged Hilfenhaus through to Haddin. Tremlett and Anderson quickly followed, bowled by Hilfenhaus and Siddle respectively, but the masterful Trott remained immovable at the other end. By the end of England's innings, Trott had defied Australia's bowlers for over eight hours. He would rightfully go on to collect the man-of-the-match award.

Australia were faced with a staggering deficit of 415 runs as they came out to bat for a second time, with eight sessions of the match still remaining. Watson and Hughes made a positive start and took less than 10 overs to post 50, but their hard work was swiftly undone as Hughes was run out for 23 after reacting slowly to his partner's call for a risky single.

The tourists exerted tremendous pressure thereafter but had to wait until the afternoon session to enjoy further success. It was Bresnan who provided the inspiration, the burly seamer trapping Watson lbw for 54 before bowling Ponting via an inside edge as Australia's skipper played with an angled bat. As if that was not enough, Bresnan then removed Hussey for a duck with the help of a superb reflex catch from Bell, who

> **"Absolutely I still want to be captain. I still feel I have a whole lot to offer the team as far as batting and leadership is concerned."**
> **RICKY PONTING**

79

moved sharply to his right at short cover. More than a few eyebrows had been raised at the start of the match when Bresnan was picked ahead of Finn, the leading wicket-taker in the series, but, in claiming three scalps in the space of 18 balls, the Yorkshireman could not have done more to back up his selection.

Clarke and Smith added a painstaking 30 for the fifth wicket before the vice-captain was caught at second slip off Swann, who conceded just 23 runs from his 22 overs on day three. Smith then played on to Anderson shortly before the close to ensure Australia ended the day on 169 for six and with Harris unable to bat, England required only three wickets to claim victory.

The first of those arrived quickly on the fourth morning as Tremlett bowled Johnson via inside edge and pad for six. Haddin and Siddle delayed the inevitable with an entertaining alliance of 86, Siddle surpassing his highest Test score in the process, but their efforts counted for little. Siddle was eventually removed by Swann for 40 as he looked to claim a second six off the spinner, a leaping Pietersen making no mistake at long-on. Swann had claimed the final wicket of the 2009 Ashes, but on this occasion it was to be Bresnan who brought proceedings to an end as he had Hilfenhaus caught behind for a duck.

Haddin was left stranded on 55 for Australia and sank to his knees in despair as his side's inevitable defeat was confirmed. Their hopes of reclaiming the urn had vanished, but England were not finished yet and headed to Sydney determined to seal a series win.

Ricky Ponting's last involvement in the series as he is bowled by Tim Bresnan before missing the final Test.

Man of the moment
Jonathan Trott lifts his bat
to acknowledge a standing
ovation from the MCG
crowd after running out
of partners and finishing
unbeaten on 168 as England
posted a mammoth 513 all
out in their first innings
to establish a match-
winning lead.

Down and out
Ricky Ponting is comprehensively dismissed by Tim Bresnan (above) during the second innings and (right) Australia's problems continued in the field when Ryan Harris suffered an injury to his left ankle and took no further part in the match.

Shining star
Alastair Cook gets to work on the ball in his role as England's polisher-in-chief. The England seamers' ability to produce reverse swing proved to be one of the major differences between the two teams.

"I do like the big occasion, and I do like being under pressure – I think it brings out the best in me."
TIM BRESNAN

84

Celebration time

Matt Prior (above), Paul
Collingwood (right) and
captain Andrew Strauss (left),
with a broken model of the
urn, celebrate retaining the
Ashes on Australian soil for
the first time in 24 years.

"*Winning the Ashes in Australia has always been a
bit of a Holy Grail for English sides.*"
ANDREW STRAUSS

85

Let's dance

Graeme Swann's "sprinkler" dance was one of the more unusual talking points of the series. He is joined by the rest of the England team in performing it in front of the delighted Barmy Army after the tourists went 2-1 up in the series.

FINAL SCORECARD

Fourth Test, Melbourne
26, 27, 28, 29 December 2010
England won the toss and elected to bowl

AUSTRALIA

1ST INNS			R	B	4	6	M
SR Watson .... c Pietersen	b Tremlett		5	12	0	0	15
PJ Hughes .... c Pietersen	b Bresnan		16	32	2	0	61
RT Ponting * .... c Swann	b Tremlett		10	38	2	0	51
MJ Clarke .... c Prior	b Anderson		20	54	2	0	88
MEK Hussey .... c Prior	b Anderson		8	41	1	0	45
SPD Smith .... c Prior	b Anderson		6	15	0	0	17
BJ Haddin + ... c Strauss	b Bresnan		5	16	1	0	22
MG Johnson .... c Prior	b Anderson		0	4	0	0	7
RJ Harris .... not out			10	23	2	0	38
PM Siddle .... c Prior	b Tremlett		11	15	1	0	23
BW Hilfenhaus .... c Prior	b Tremlett		0	8	0	0	10
Extras	(b 0, lb 2, w 0, nb 5)		7				
TOTAL			98				

BOWLING	O	M	R	W
Anderson	16	4	44	4
Tremlett	11.5	5	26	4
Bresnan	13	6	25	2
Swann	2	1	1	0

2ND INNS			R	B	4	6	M
SR Watson .... lbw	b Bresnan		54	102	7	0	136
PJ Hughes .... run out (Trott)			23	30	2	0	49
RT Ponting *	b Bresnan		20	73	2	0	101
MJ Clarke .... c Strauss	b Swann		13	66	0	0	81
MEK Hussey .... c Bell	b Bresnan		0	7	0	0	8
SPD Smith	b Anderson		38	67	6	0	90
BJ Haddin + ... not out			55	93	4	1	135
MG Johnson	b Tremlett		6	22	0	0	23
PM Siddle .... c Pietersen	b Swann		40	50	5	1	68
BW Hilfenhaus .... c Prior	b Bresnan		0	4	0	0	5
RJ Harris .... absent hurt							
Extras	(b 1, lb 6, w 2, nb 0)		9				
TOTAL			258				

BOWLING	O	M	R	W
Anderson	20	1	71	1
Tremlett	17	3	71	1
Bresnan	21.4	8	50	4
Swann	27	11	59	2

ENGLAND

1ST INNS			R	B	4	6	M
AJ Strauss * .... c Hussey	b Siddle		69	167	5	0	228
AN Cook .... c Watson	b Siddle		82	152	11	0	208
IJL Trott .... not out			168	345	14	0	482
KP Pietersen .... lbw	b Siddle		51	89	7	0	125
PD Collingwood ...... c Siddle	b Johnson		8	15	1	0	27
IR Bell .... c Siddle	b Johnson		1	13	0	0	20
MJ Prior + ... c Ponting	b Siddle		85	119	11	0	197
TT Bresnan .... c Haddin	b Siddle		4	17	0	0	21
GP Swann .... c Haddin	b Hilfenhaus		22	28	3	0	50
CT Tremlett	b Hilfenhaus		4	7	0	0	7
JM Anderson	b Siddle		1	6	0	0	4
Extras	(b 10, lb 2, w 3, nb 3)		18				
TOTAL			513				

BOWLING	O	M	R	W
Hilfenhaus	37	13	83	2
Harris	28.4	9	91	0
Johnson	29	2	134	2
Siddle	33.1	10	75	6
Watson	10	1	34	0
Smith	18	3	71	0
Clarke.....................	3.2	0	13	0

FALL OF WICKETS

	AUS 1st inns	ENG 1st inns	AUS 2nd inns
1st............................	15	159	53
2nd...........................	37	170	99
3rd............................	37	262	102
4th............................	58	281	104
5th............................	66	286	134
6th............................	77	459	158
7th............................	77	465	172
8th............................	77	508	258
9th............................	92	512	258
10th..........................	98	513	

ENGLAND WON BY AN INNINGS AND 157 RUNS

Umpires: Aleem Dar and AL Hill

* captain + wicketkeeper

The decision to bring in Tim Bresnan immediately paid dividends as he took six wickets in the match, including four for 50 in Australia's second innings.

88

MAN OF THE MATCH
Jonathan Trott

It speaks volumes for Jonathan Trott's batting effort in Melbourne that he received the man-of-the-match award despite England's bowlers blowing Australia away for 98 on the opening day.

The need for the tourists to capitalise on their exploits with the ball was all the more important given the way in which they had let an excellent first-day position slip in Perth.

The stage seemed set for a Kevin Pietersen masterclass, or a fluent captain's century from Andrew Strauss. Both men did register 50s, but it was Trott who stole the show with a perfect display of old-fashioned Test batsmanship.

In their number three, England have found a man with an insatiable appetite for runs.

That hunger was more evident than ever as he reached his third Ashes century in five Tests, displaying determination and class in a

"This is definitely an important Test match and one I'll savour. They're all pretty special. But Boxing Day, with the hype around it and the support from the English fans, it would definitely be right up there."
JONATHAN TROTT

chanceless 486-minute stay at the crease. By the time Trott walked back to the pavilion with his bat aloft, having excelled on the biggest stage of all – the Boxing Day Test at the MCG – England held a first-innings lead of 415 and an Ashes-retaining victory was a near certainty.

89

Fifth Test
Sydney

3–7 JANUARY 2011

The Ashes may have already been retained, but England still had plenty to play for at the SCG. If they avoided defeat, Andrew Strauss's side would become the first set of tourists in 24 years to win the Ashes outright in Australia.

6

Fifth Test Sydney

England subjected Australia to further agony as they wrapped up a 3-1 series win in Sydney. The tourists' domination was once again displayed in the clearest possible fashion as they sauntered to an innings-and-83-run triumph. Alastair Cook rounded off a sensational individual tour with a masterful 189, but each and every one of England's players had reason to feel proud after the most satisfying of victories.

England rounded off an historic Ashes campaign in sensational style at the SCG with another commanding win.

As a result of their triumph in the final Test, the tourists followed in the footsteps of Mike Gatting's 1986–87 side, the last England team to claim a series victory Down Under, and their success is sure to live long in the memory of those who witnessed it.

For the third time in five matches, Australia were thoroughly outplayed from start to finish as they slumped to an innings-and-83-run defeat. Michael Clarke deputised as captain in the absence of the injured Ricky Ponting, but he could do nothing to inspire an upturn in fortunes.

Fittingly, it was Alastair Cook and James Anderson, England's leading performers throughout the series, who made the most significant

Australia's tailenders held England up in the first innings as a half-century from Mitchell Johnson (right) and defiant support from fellow seamer Ben Hilfenhaus (far right) added much-needed runs.

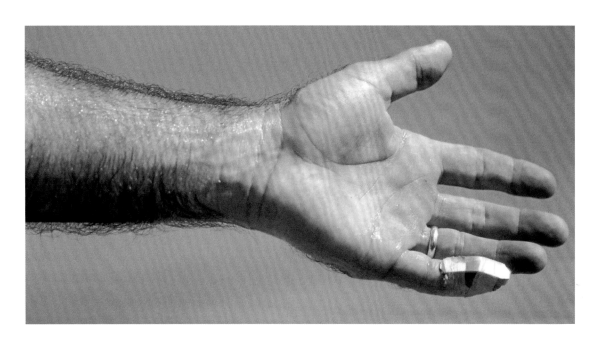

The splint on Ricky Ponting's injured finger which forced him to miss the final Test, with Michael Clarke taking over as Australia captain.

contributions with bat and ball in Sydney. Cook compiled a majestic 189, taking his run tally for the series to a staggering 766, while Anderson claimed seven victims in the match to underline his position as the leading bowler on either side.

Four of the Lancashire seamer's wickets came in the first innings as Australia were bowled out for 280, despite useful lower-order contributions from Mitchell Johnson and Ben Hilfenhaus. The game looked to be in the balance as England slipped to 226 for five in reply, but Ian Bell and Matt Prior duly registered their first Ashes hundreds to end any hope of a home win.

England went on to reach 644 – their highest total in Australia – and from then on it was a matter of when, not if, they would secure victory. Their moment of glory arrived on the fifth morning, Chris Tremlett bowling Michael Beer to dismiss the hosts for 281.

The match provided Paul Collingwood with the perfect send-off after the Durham veteran announced his retirement from Test cricket ahead of the fourth day's play. Collingwood was unable to bow out with a big score, but he did pick up the key first-innings wicket of Mike Hussey in his final act as a bowler.

Australia's top-order had displayed a lack of application in Melbourne, so it was no surprise to see openers Shane Watson and Phil Hughes adopt a more cautious approach after Clarke had won the toss and elected to bat first on his home ground. There was plenty of early assistance for the bowlers on a surface laced with green, but Watson and Hughes battled gamely in a morning session that yielded only 55 runs.

England were rewarded for their accuracy and discipline in the final over before lunch as Hughes edged a back-of-a-length delivery from Tremlett into the hands of Collingwood at third slip. The left-hander had showed admirable patience in grinding his way to 31 and his frustration was evident as he trudged from the crease.

With Ponting unavailable, Usman Khawaja was handed an opportunity to shine at number three and the debutant wasted little time in making a positive impression, pulling his second ball for four in emphatic fashion. He and Watson had moved the score on to 92 by the time bad light forced the players off for a brief period in the afternoon, but Watson fell for 45 shortly after the resumption, caught at first slip by Andrew Strauss off the dependable Tim Bresnan.

An early tea was taken following a further stoppage, this time for rain, and only 11.1 overs were possible before more showers signalled the end of play. By that stage, Australia had slumped to 134 for four, with Clarke and Khawaja back in the pavilion.

The stand-in skipper made only four before cutting Bresnan straight to Anderson at gully, while Khawaja's promising innings ended on 37 as he was dismissed by the last delivery of the day. With the rain about to return, the youngster attempted to sweep Graeme Swann and succeeded only in finding a back-pedalling Jonathan Trott at square leg.

England enjoyed additional success early on the second morning when Brad Haddin chased a wide ball from Anderson and edged behind on the back foot. Hussey and Steven Smith then shared an assiduous partnership of 28, but the former departed to the final ball of the 80th over as he played on to the gentle medium-pace of Collingwood, thus exposing the tail to the new ball.

Anderson took full advantage by having Smith and Siddle caught in the slips and a score of 200 appeared likely to prove beyond Australia before Johnson and Hilfenhaus came to their rescue. Deciding that the best form of defence was attack, the duo found the boundary with regularity and added 76 for the ninth wicket in fewer than 15 overs.

Johnson was eventually bowled by Bresnan for 53 and the innings was brought to an end when Hilfenhaus, on 34, edged Anderson through to Prior. The home side had regained valuable momentum, but they were soon on the back foot again as Strauss got England off to a flier in reply.

Aided by some dreadful bowling, Strauss collected seven fours and a six in a 49-ball half-century, his quickest in Test cricket, and dominated an opening stand of 98 with Cook before being bowled by Hilfenhaus.

Trott failed to reproduce his Melbourne heroics and fell for a duck when he played on to Johnson, but Cook had another substantial score in his

"It means everything. Earlier in my career I was pretty much outdone by Australia. Hopefully I can kick on."
IAN BELL ON HIS MAIDEN ASHES CENTURY

England centurions (from left) Alastair Cook, Ian Bell and Matt Prior all raise their bats to acknowledge the applause of the crowd after helping the tourists post their highest total in Australia.

sights and settled England nerves alongside Kevin Pietersen.

An uncharacteristic lapse in concentration almost cost the Essex man his wicket on 46 as he aimed an unsightly heave at Beer and was caught at mid-on. However, Australia's newest spinner was denied a maiden Test scalp as umpire Billy Bowden called for a replay, which proved the bowler had overstepped.

Cook subsequently progressed to 50 and Pietersen looked set to achieve a similar feat, only to throw his wicket away in careless fashion. A short ball from Johnson was top-edged to Beer at deep backward square and England ended the day on 167 for three, still trailing by 113.

Siddle picked up the wicket of nightwatchman Anderson on the third morning before a controversial incident sparked further frustration for Beer. Cook was on 99 when he turned the debut spinner to Hughes at short leg, who initially appeared reluctant to celebrate the dismissal as enthusiastically as his team-mates. The reason for his hesitation soon became clear as, with the batsman standing his ground, the umpires called for video evidence, which proved conclusively that the ball had bounced.

The episode prompted mutterings from many, but Cook remained unflustered and brought up his third hundred of the series, from 202 deliveries. To his credit, Beer also responded well and finally picked up a deserved first wicket as Collingwood, in what would prove to be his final

Umpire Billy Bowden's famous crooked finger signals the end for opener Phil Hughes in Australia's second innings.

> "I can't think of a better way to bow out of Test cricket. There are some great guys in that dressing room and this feels very special."
> PAUL COLLINGWOOD

Test innings, attempted to go over the top and was caught by Hilfenhaus at mid-on for 13.

England were 54 runs in arrears at the time of Collingwood's departure, but Cook and Bell batted with calmness and no little elegance to take the game away from Australia, the opener surpassing a host of records in the process. An attractive partnership of 154 was ultimately ended in the third over after tea, Cook falling 11 runs short of a double hundred as he sliced Watson to Hussey at gully.

Bell almost followed in Watson's next set of six, but the Warwickshire batsman managed to successfully overturn a caught-behind verdict, with the umpires unable to call on the "Snicko" technology that eventually suggested there had been an inside edge.

Bell made the most of his reprieve by completing his first Test hundred against Australia, a hugely significant milestone given his previous struggles against England's Ashes rivals. He was removed by Johnson, for 115, shortly before the end of day three, but not before adding 107 for the seventh wicket with an attack-minded Prior, who reached the close unbeaten on 54.

England's lead stood at 208, but if Australia thought things could not get any worse, they were sorely mistaken as runs flowed with embarrassing ease on the fourth morning. Prior exhibited great fluency en route to a sparkling 118, which came from just 130 balls, while Bresnan and Swann rubbed salt into the wounds of a demoralised attack with 35 and 36 respectively. Johnson finished as the leading wicket-taker in the innings, but his four scalps came at a cost of 168 runs, with 20 being taken from his final over alone.

Just as in Melbourne, Watson and Hughes returned to the middle with their side facing a mammoth deficit and they once again saw off the new ball before suffering another calamitous run-out. Watson had taken responsibility for running his partner out in the previous match, but he contributed to his own downfall on this occasion as he ignored Hughes and hared through for a second run that was never available. The two batsmen found themselves together at the non-striker's end as Prior collected a throw from Pietersen and gleefully whipped off the bails, one of many ignominious moments on a humiliating day for Australia.

Steven Smith held England up on the final day as he slogged his way to an unbeaten if ungainly half-century, but it was only delaying the inevitable outcome.

Bresnan made a second breakthrough for England when he ousted Hughes for 13 and, although a partnership of 65 followed, the tourists continued their inexorable push for victory by claiming a flurry of wickets late in the day.

The collapse was triggered by Anderson, who induced Khawaja and Clarke to edge behind during another incisive spell of swing bowling. Hussey was then caught at gully to give Bresnan his second wicket before Tremlett took centre stage with two wickets in as many balls, Haddin nicking through to Prior and Johnson beaten for pace by a searing delivery that crashed into the stumps.

Strauss claimed the extra half-hour in a bid to wrap up proceedings at the earliest possible opportunity, but Smith and Siddle held firm and showed no shortage of courage in taking their partnership to 86 when play resumed on the final morning.

A brief rain delay provided further irritation for England, but that would soon be forgotten as the final three wickets fell in quick succession. Swann had Siddle caught in the deep by Anderson, who then located Hilfenhaus's edge to claim his 24th wicket of the series.

It was to be Tremlett who delivered the final blow, bowling Beer via a bottom edge to write his name into Ashes folklore and spark scenes of unbridled jubilation.

> "England have outplayed us through this series, in all facets of the game."
> MICHAEL CLARKE

FIFTH TEST

Pretty in pink

The SCG was transformed into a sea of pink in support of the Jane McGrath Foundation. The charity was set up to fund research into breast cancer following the death of the wife of former Australia fast bowler Glenn McGrath (above right, with Kevin Pietersen). Fans and players got into the spirit, with the home side wearing 'Baggy Pinks' (left) in the build-up to the game.

"It goes to show what is possible; everybody turns up in pink and, if you don't, you feel out of place. It just goes to show what's possible and how you can create awareness out of something that was pretty tough."
GLENN MCGRATH

100

"Jonathan Trott said to me 'it's the best feeling in cricket' and I'd have to agree. An Ashes ton is very, very special and I'll treasure it."
MATT PRIOR ON HIS MAIDEN ASHES CENTURY

On the run
Clockwise from left: Kevin Pietersen celebrates running out opener Shane Watson in Australia's second innings; Mitchell Johnson's body language in the field sums up Australia's sinking feeling; Matt Prior hits out on his way to a maiden Ashes century.

"Now we have done it, I think we can give a big sigh of relief and be very proud of what we have achieved, because not many sides have come out here and won – and certainly not many as emphatically as we did."
ANDREW STRAUSS

That winning feeling
Clockwise from right: England players join together to celebrate completing an historic victory and shake hands with their beaten opponents before captain Andrew Strauss cherishes winning the famous urn once again.

103

FINAL SCORECARD
Fifth Test, Sydney
3, 4, 5, 6, 7 January 2011
Australia won the toss and elected to bat

AUSTRALIA

1ST INNS

			R	B	4	6	M
SR Watson	c Strauss	b Bresnan	45	127	5	0	193
PJ Hughes	c Collingwood	b Tremlett	31	93	5	0	122
UT Khawaja	c Trott	b Swann	37	95	5	0	136
MJ Clarke *	c Anderson	b Bresnan	4	21	0	0	33
MEK Hussey		b Collingwood	33	92	2	0	176
BJ Haddin +	c Prior	b Anderson	6	13	0	0	13
SPD Smith	c Collingwood	b Anderson	18	53	1	0	86
MG Johnson		b Bresnan	53	66	5	1	88
PM Siddle	c Strauss	b Anderson	2	4	0	0	2
BW Hilfenhaus	c Prior	b Anderson	34	58	3	1	88
MA Beer	not out		2	17	0	0	23
Extras	(b 5, lb 7, w 1, nb 2)		15				
TOTAL			280				

BOWLING

	O	M	R	W
Anderson	30.1	7	66	4
Tremlett	26	9	71	1
Bresnan	30	5	89	3
Swann	16	4	37	1
Collingwood	4	2	5	1

2ND INNS

			R	B	4	6	M
SR Watson	run out (Pietersen)		38	40	7	0	51
PJ Hughes	c Prior	b Bresnan	13	58	1	0	75
UT Khawaja	c Prior	b Anderson	21	73	2	0	85
MJ Clarke *	c Prior	b Anderson	41	73	6	0	92
MEK Hussey	c Pietersen	b Bresnan	12	49	1	0	65
BJ Haddin +	c Prior	b Tremlett	30	41	3	0	50
SPD Smith	not out		54	90	6	0	160
MG Johnson		b Tremlett	0	1	0	0	0
PM Siddle	c Anderson	b Swann	43	65	4	0	114
BW Hilfenhaus	c Prior	b Anderson	7	11	1	0	13
MA Beer		b Tremlett	2	9	0	0	14
Extras	(b 11, lb 4, w 3, nb 2)		20				
TOTAL			281				

BOWLING

	O	M	R	W
Anderson	18	5	61	3
Tremlett	20.4	4	79	3
Bresnan	18	6	51	2
Swann	28	8	75	1

ENGLAND

1ST INNS

			R	B	4	6	M
AJ Strauss *		b Hilfenhaus	60	58	8	1	91
AN Cook	c Hussey	b Watson	189	342	16	0	484
IJL Trott		b Johnson	0	6	0	0	5
KP Pietersen	c Beer	b Johnson	36	70	4	0	86
JM Anderson		b Siddle	7	35	1	0	38
PD Collingwood	c Hilfenhaus	b Beer	13	41	0	0	68
IR Bell	c Clarke	b Johnson	115	232	13	0	292
MJ Prior +	c Haddin	b Hilfenhaus	118	130	11	1	233
TT Bresnan	c Clarke	b Johnson	35	103	5	0	112
GP Swann	not out		36	26	3	1	48
CT Tremlett	c Haddin	b Hilfenhaus	12	28	1	0	34
Extras	(b 3, lb 11, w 5, nb 4)		23				
TOTAL			644				

BOWLING

	O	M	R	W
Hilfenhaus	38.5	7	121	3
Johnson	36	5	168	4
Siddle	31	5	111	1
Watson	20	7	49	1
Beer	38	3	112	1
Smith	13	0	67	0
Hussey	1	0	2	0

James Anderson's seven wickets in the final Test at Sydney took his tally to 24 for the series.

FALL OF WICKETS

	AUS 1st inns	ENG 1st inns	AUS 2nd inns
1st	55	98	46
2nd	105	99	52
3rd	113	165	117
4th	134	181	124
5th	143	226	161
6th	171	380	171
7th	187	487	171
8th	189	589	257
9th	265	609	267
10th	280	644	281

ENGLAND WON BY AN INNINGS AND 83 RUNS
Umpires: Aleem Dar and BF Bowden
* captain + wicketkeeper

MAN OF THE MATCH
Alastair Cook

Having delivered in every game except Perth, there was little more for Alastair Cook to prove by the time the final Test came around.

Heading to Sydney, the opener already had a scarcely believable 577 runs to his name and the man-of-the-series award was practically wrapped up.

Yet, for Cook, there was unfinished business. Unprepared to rest on his laurels, the Essex man produced arguably his most fluent innings of the tour as he hit the ball to all parts during his 342-ball stay. His eventual total of 189 was his second highest in Tests – bettered only by his exploits at Brisbane – but it was his crease occupation that was again so impressive.

By spending another 488 minutes in the middle, he took his tally for the series to

> "I spent a lot of last summer not scoring runs. It's pretty lonely. When you don't get any for a while, then you find form, you've got to make the most of it."
> **ALASTAIR COOK**

2,171, the most by any batsman in a five-Test campaign. More importantly, his effort set an excellent platform from which England posted a first-innings score of 644.

Victory was a formality thereafter and no man had done more than Cook in helping the tourists to a 3-1 series win.

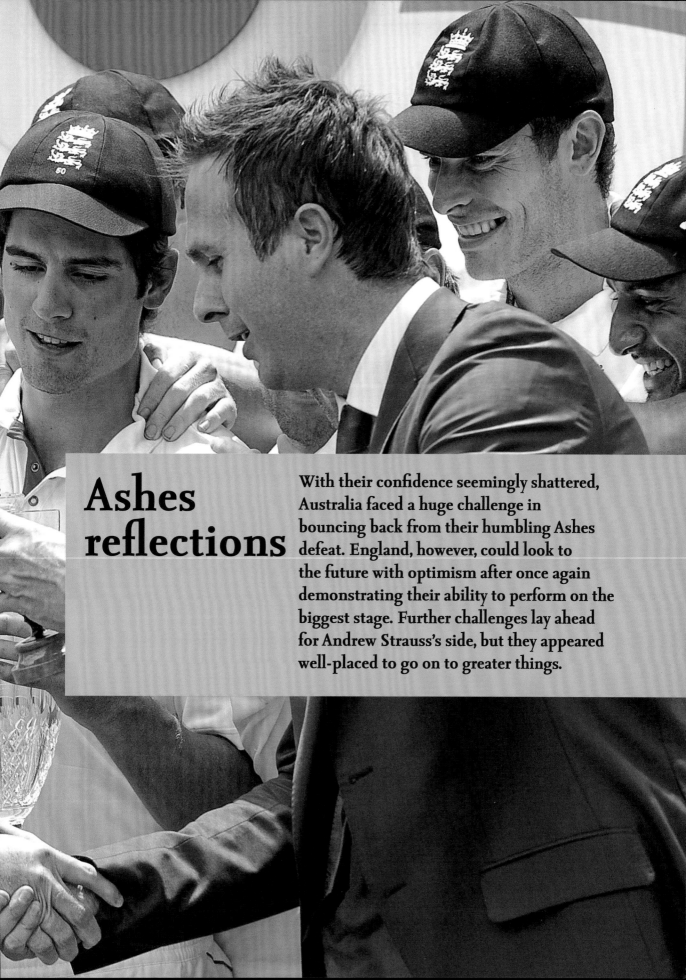

Ashes reflections

With their confidence seemingly shattered, Australia faced a huge challenge in bouncing back from their humbling Ashes defeat. England, however, could look to the future with optimism after once again demonstrating their ability to perform on the biggest stage. Further challenges lay ahead for Andrew Strauss's side, but they appeared well-placed to go on to greater things.

7 Ashes reflections

It was hardly surprising to see Australia come in for heavy criticism in the wake of England's comprehensive Ashes victory. The hosts had been outplayed for much of the series and had few positives to take as they contemplated their next step. That was not the case for England, although team director Andy Flower was quick to ensure his jubilant side remained focused as they looked to climb the ICC Test rankings.

It had been clear for some time that Australia were no longer the dominant force they once were, but the 2010–11 Ashes provided a dramatic illustration of just how far they had fallen.

Ahead of England's arrival Down Under, a bullish Mike Hussey had responded confidently to questions about his side's lowly position of fifth in the ICC Test rankings.

"I don't think that's a true reflection of our team," insisted the veteran batsman. "We're definitely better than that."

By the time the tourists had wrapped up a comprehensive 3-1 victory, it was hard to agree with such an appraisal, despite the valiant efforts of Hussey himself, who finished as the second-highest run-scorer in the series behind Alastair Cook.

After all, Australia were not only beaten by England, they suffered humiliating innings defeats on three occasions. For a country accustomed to routine Ashes triumphs on home soil, it was the most jarring of wake-up calls.

"This is probably as close to rock bottom as it gets," admitted Michael Clarke after the final Test in Sydney, where he deputised as captain in

"This is probably as close to rock bottom as it gets. We have no excuses. We need to go back to the drawing board and work our backsides off."
MICHAEL CLARKE

The celebrations begin and the famous Ashes urn is in English hands once again.

place of the injured Ricky Ponting. "We have no excuses. We need to go back to the drawing board and work our backsides off."

While Australia clearly had plenty to ponder, England were able to revel in the sweetest of successes after finally ending their long wait for a series victory Down Under. Andrew Strauss's side had proven they no longer feared facing their oldest rivals on their own turf, a point emphasised by the skipper when he declared: "I think we were as confident as I've ever seen an England team."

Strauss and his team-mates had every reason to be satisfied with their efforts, particularly after Australia had eased to a 5-0 Test series whitewash on England's last tour there. "It's extra special for the guys who were here last time, definitely," said team director Andy Flower. "To come back from that shows a lot of character on their part."

Yet although they were understandably jubilant, England were well aware that they had yet to achieve their primary goal of becoming the leading side in world cricket.

Following his side's series-clinching win at the SCG, a typically composed Flower explained: "We must look back on this with pride and satisfaction but there will be a moment to draw a line and move on."

Flower's message emphasised the changing fortunes of England and Australia. As the home side wallowed in the misery of an unexpectedly heavy defeat, their opponents were already switching their focus to the next challenge. After storming to Ashes glory in such sensational fashion, it remained to be seen just how far England could go.

Job done
Chris Tremlett celebrates bowling Australia's last man, Michael Beer, in the second innings in Sydney, and the series is over.

112

Mixed emotions

While Alastair Cook, Graeme Swann and James Anderson (right), and Tim Bresnan (below right) celebrate a job well done in the Sydney changing room, the Australian players (bottom right) can only look on with rueful reflections.

"We must look back on this with pride and satisfaction but there will be a moment to draw a line and move on."
ANDY FLOWER

113

114

"The Barmy Army have been fantastic throughout this trip and have made a lot of Australian grounds feel like home for us."
JAMES ANDERSON

Occupying force

England's eccentric and passionate band of followers, the Barmy Army, provided the backdrop to historic scenes throughout the tour, and earned the thanks of England favourite Graeme Swann (left).

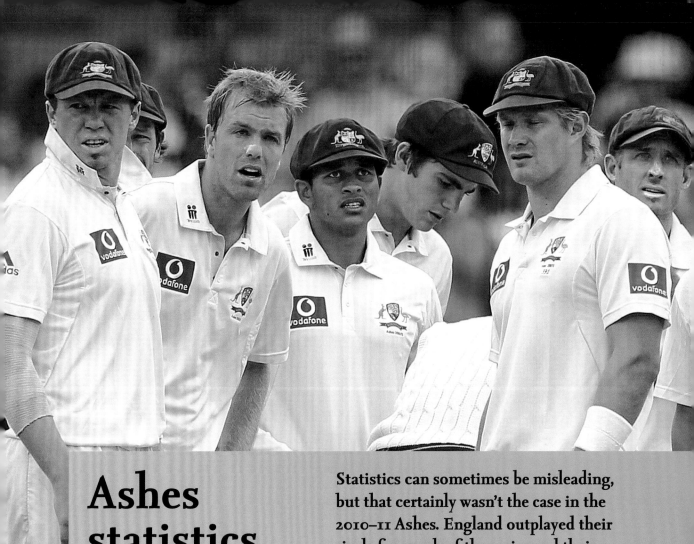

Ashes statistics

Statistics can sometimes be misleading, but that certainly wasn't the case in the 2010–11 Ashes. England outplayed their rivals for much of the series and their dominance was reflected in the batting and bowling averages. Ricky Ponting was among the high-profile names to struggle for Australia as they sank to an unexpectedly heavy defeat.

How they rated
Australia

As the series progressed it became clear that Australia's team contained too many players who were out of form. Mike Hussey and Shane Watson performed admirably throughout and the seam attack flourished in Perth, but for the majority of the series England were simply too good. Australia's selectors chopped and changed in search of a winning formula, with 17 players eventually featuring across the five Tests.

RICKY PONTING (CAPTAIN) 2/10
Tasmania, Age 36, Tests 152, right-hand bat
Ponting could hardly have imagined a more miserable series. His runs return was unfathomably poor for one of the world's best batsmen, and he suffered a broken finger in Perth that would eventually rule him out of the final Test and require surgery.

MICHAEL CLARKE (VICE-CAPTAIN) 4/10
New South Wales, Age 29, Tests 69, right-hand bat, slow left-arm bowler
Fared only marginally better than Ponting with the bat, with his only notable contribution a defiant 80 in Adelaide, which ultimately proved in vain. Was shunted into the captaincy in unenviable circumstances in Sydney and failed to inspire a change in fortunes.

MICHAEL BEER 5/10
Western Australia, Age 26, Tests 1, right-hand bat, slow left-arm bowler
Twice thought he had Alastair Cook as his maiden Test wicket in Sydney, before Paul Collingwood's wicket got him started instead. Beer appeared to have been chosen from a pretty bare cupboard, but nevertheless gave a solid debut performance.

DOUG BOLLINGER 3/10
New South Wales, Age 29, Tests 12, left-hand bat, left-arm fast-medium bowler
Drafted in for the second Test in Adelaide, but appeared short of full fitness. After picking up the early wicket of Andrew Strauss, Bollinger failed to impress and finished the match with disappointing figures of one for 130 from his 29 overs.

XAVIER DOHERTY 2/10
Tasmania, Age 28, Tests 2, left-hand bat, slow left-arm bowler

Doherty received a shock call-up for the first Test but did little to justify his selection. Things were to get worse for the newcomer in Adelaide. He did pick up the prized wicket of Kevin Pietersen, but only after the batsman had made 227.

BRAD HADDIN 8/10
New South Wales, Age 33, Tests 32, right-hand bat, wicketkeeper

Set a false tone for the series in his triple-century stand with Mike Hussey in Brisbane, but remained one of his team's few reliable batsmen. A close call between him and Matt Prior as to who would make a composite XI – a compliment to both.

RYAN HARRIS 7/10
Queensland, Age 31, Tests 5, right-hand bat, right-arm fast-medium bowler

Harris will never fail for lack of effort, but he is notoriously vulnerable to injury, as he proved again when he broke down in Melbourne after bowling more than 80 Test overs in around three weeks. He is Australia's most consistent pace bowler, when fit.

BEN HILFENHAUS 4/10
Tasmania, Age 27, Tests 17, right-hand bat, right-arm medium-fast bowler

A classic English-conditions swing bowler, the snag for Hilfenhaus is that he is Australian. He lacked the cutting edge to seriously trouble England's top order but might easily have picked up a few more wickets with a little more fortune.

Australia had all too few causes for celebration during the series, and selection changes meant they used 17 different players in five matches.

119

PHIL HUGHES 3/10
New South Wales, Age 22, Tests 10, left-hand bat
The diminutive opener appears to have adapted his one-dimensional and idiosyncractic technique to a degree. But it is remarkable that a batsman with so few favoured scoring areas has gone so far so quickly, and the jury must stay out about the likely length of his Test career.

MIKE HUSSEY 9/10
Western Australia, Age 35, Tests 59, left-hand bat
Without Hussey, Australia would have been sunk without trace long before Melbourne. Only Cook could top him for runs, after both began the series with only a tenuous hold on their place in the side. The Western Australian proved the adage that class is permanent.

MITCHELL JOHNSON 5/10
Western Australia, Age 29, Tests 42, left-hand bat, left-arm fast bowler
Famously blows very hot or very cold. Endured a nightmare first Test, was dropped for the second and then almost single-handedly won the third. Johnson did not quite go to those extremes in Melbourne or Sydney, but Australia badly need more consistency from him.

Opening batsman Phil Hughes is still to convince critics that he is suited to Test cricket.

SIMON KATICH 5/10

New South Wales, Age 35, Tests 56, left-hand bat, left-arm chinaman bowler

Badly missed by Australia after his Achilles injury in Adelaide. Katich failed to hit top form in the opening two Tests but would surely have made more runs than his replacement Hughes had he featured in the remainder of the series.

USMAN KHAWAJA 6/10

New South Wales, Age 24, Tests 1, left-hand bat

Could find no way past under-performing colleagues until Sydney. He did enough there to suggest he has a major Test career in front of him, although the over-reaction to the left-hander's first-innings 37 spoke volumes about Australia's problems.

Usman Khawaja made a good impression when he finally got to make his Test debut in the final Test in Sydney.

MARCUS NORTH 3/10

Western Australia, Age 31, Tests 21, left-hand bat, right-arm off-spin bowler

A notable weak link in a team featuring a host of out-of-form players. North did not survive the cut after the second-Test defeat and could have few complaints after making only 49 runs in his three innings.

PETER SIDDLE 7/10

Victoria, Age 26, Tests 22, right-hand bat, right-arm fast-medium

Justified his questionable presence in the first Test with a hat-trick on his birthday, which meant England had to dig deep to escape with a draw. A captain's dream, because he just keeps running in, Siddle needs others to pull their weight around him too.

STEVE SMITH 4/10

New South Wales, Age 21, Tests 5, right-hand bat, leg-spin bowler

Did not show nearly enough with the bat to explain the high regard in which he is held, until a defiant half-century with the cause well and truly lost in Sydney. His leg-spin is not international class either at this stage.

SHANE WATSON 8/10

Queensland, Age 29, Tests 27, right-hand bat, right-arm medium-fast bowler

One of the few batting bankers in a woefully brittle line-up, although many quibble about the once makeshift opener's inability to convert 50s into hundreds. Watson's disciplined medium pace also gives his team an admirable balance.

Ages and Test appearances correct as of 7 January 2011, the final day of the Ashes series

How they rated
England

England's players knew they would need to be on top of their game if they were to achieve a long-awaited Test series win in Australia and they rose to the challenge magnificently. Although certain individuals performed particularly well, the tourists' success came as a result of notable contributions from each of the 13 players who took the field during the series. Team director Andy Flower could not have asked for more.

ANDREW STRAUSS (CAPTAIN) 8/10
Middlesex, Age 33, Tests 82, left-hand bat
Led a happy group of tourists with his trademark calm authority and joins an elite band of English captains to have enjoyed Ashes success Down Under. Strauss had a solid series with the bat and finished with 307 runs at an average of 43.85.

ALASTAIR COOK (VICE-CAPTAIN) 10/10
Essex, Age 26, Tests 65, left-hand bat
Began the tour with his position under question, but spent most of it acknowledging cheers for his prolific run-making. Surpassing all but Wally Hammond in England's list of top scorers in an Ashes series, Cook was the single biggest reason for England's success.

JAMES ANDERSON 9/10
Lancashire, Age 28, Tests 57, left-hand bat, right-arm fast-medium bowler
The series' top wicket-taker proved all the doubters wrong. Anderson very nearly deserves to share top billing with Cook after showing that he does not necessarily need cloud cover and clumps of grass on a length to be a world-class seam and swing bowler.

IAN BELL 8/10
Warwickshire, Age 28, Tests 62, right-hand bat
Bell's talent has never been in doubt, but the Warwickshire batsman knew he had a point to prove after previous struggles against Australia. He answered his critics in emphatic fashion and richly deserved his first Ashes hundred in Sydney.

TIM BRESNAN 8/10

Yorkshire, Age 25, Tests 7, right-hand bat, right-arm fast-medium bowler

Bresnan exceeded all expectations apart, perhaps, from his own, with six wickets in Melbourne after being called up to replace Steven Finn. He exploited conditions wonderfully well there and adapted skilfully again in Sydney to further demonstrate his worth.

STUART BROAD 5/10

Notts, Age 24, Tests 34, left-hand bat, right-arm fast-medium bowler

It seemed a major blow to England when Broad's abdominal injury ended his tour after two Tests, but the tourists had greater strength in depth than many imagined. The seamer was unfortunate not to claim more than two wickets after bowling with great control.

PAUL COLLINGWOOD 4/10

Durham, Age 34, Tests 68, right-hand bat, right-arm medium bowler

Hard as he tried, Collingwood simply could not regain his batting form and duly bowed out of Test cricket in Sydney. However, he took the catch of the series to dismiss Ricky Ponting in Adelaide and provided a useful bowling option throughout the tour.

England's players could afford to smile their way round Australia as form and fitness meant they needed to use only 13 players during the series.

Conditions were rarely in Graeme Swann's favour, but the England spinner showed he can operate in a holding role just as well.

STEVEN FINN 7/10
Middlesex, Age 21, Tests 11, right-hand bat, right-arm medium-fast bowler
The tall seamer was leading on wickets but leaking runs too when England decided it was time for a rest before the final two Tests. Finn has an unflappability rarely associated with pace bowlers and can be proud of his achievements.

KEVIN PIETERSEN 7/10
Surrey, Age 30, Tests 71, right-hand bat, right-arm off-spin bowler
Pietersen answered his critics in sensational style at the Adelaide Oval, scoring a career-best 227 and also picking up the key wicket of Michael Clarke with his part-time bowling. He was kept quiet thereafter, but his confidence appears to have returned.

MATT PRIOR 8/10
Sussex, Age 28, Tests 40, right-hand bat, wicketkeeper
Prior is a good enough batsman to be an international specialist, but his wicketkeeping makes him one of the world's best all-rounders. Missed precious little behind the stumps and more than did himself justice in front of them too.

GRAEME SWANN 7/10
Notts, Age 31, Tests 29, right-hand bat, right-arm off-spin bowler
The world's number one slow bowler proved he has the nous to operate within his limitations if there is no spin. Swann still turned it on to finish off Australia in Adelaide and reverted to a supreme holding role as the seamers flourished in Melbourne.

CHRIS TREMLETT 9/10
Surrey, Age 29, Tests 6, right-hand bat, right-arm medium-fast bowler
Vindicated his selection in the Perth defeat with eight wickets on a bouncy surface, and led the effort to hustle Australia out so cheaply in the first innings in Melbourne. Tremlett was a triumph of selection for England.

JONATHAN TROTT 9/10
Warwickshire, Age 29, Tests 18, right-hand bat
Helped Cook bat for two days to salvage an all-important draw in the first Test. Trott shared another big stand with the opener in the Adelaide victory, and then showed Australia no mercy with his second unbeaten hundred of the tour at the MCG.

Ages and Test appearances correct as of 7 January 2011, the final day of the Ashes series

Ian Bell was hailed as a class act in the build-up to the series, but still had to show he could perform against Australia. Made his case emphatically with his Sydney century.

AUSTRALIA SERIES AVERAGES

BATTING

	M	I	NO	R	HS	Avg	100	50	Ct	St
MEK Hussey	5	9	0	570	195	63.33	2	3	5	-
SR Watson	5	10	1	435	95	48.33	-	4	5	-
BJ Haddin	5	9	1	360	136	45.00	1	3	8	1
SPD Smith	3	6	1	159	54*	31.80	-	1	2	-
UT Khawaja	1	2	0	58	37	29.00	-	-	-	-
SM Katich	2	4	0	97	50	24.25	-	1	1	-
MJ Clarke	5	9	0	193	80	21.44	-	1	3	-
PM Siddle	5	9	1	154	43	19.25	-	-	2	-
MG Johnson	4	7	0	122	62	17.42	-	2	-	-
MJ North	2	3	0	49	26	16.33	-	-	1	-
PJ Hughes	3	6	0	97	31	16.16	-	-	-	-
RT Ponting	4	8	1	113	51*	16.14	-	1	4	-
BW Hilfenhaus	4	7	2	55	34	11.00	-	-	1	-
XJ Doherty	2	3	0	27	16	9.00	-	-	-	-
MA Beer	1	2	1	4	2*	4.00	-	-	1	-
RJ Harris	3	5	1	14	10*	3.50	-	-	-	-
DE Bollinger	1	2	2	7	7*	-	-	-	-	-

BOWLING

	O	M	R	W	Avg	Best	5 wkt inns	10 wkt match
RJ Harris	83.4	19	281	11	25.54	6-47	1	-
PM Siddle	147.1	28	484	14	34.57	6-54	2	-
MG Johnson	136.3	22	554	15	36.93	6-38	1	-
BW Hilfenhaus	157.5	42	415	7	59.28	3-121	-	-
SR Watson	76	19	223	3	74.33	1-30	-	-
XJ Doherty	75.5	11	306	3	102.00	2-41	-	-
MJ North	38	3	110	1	110.00	1-47	-	-
MA Beer	38	3	112	1	112.00	1-112	-	-
DE Bollinger	29	1	130	1	130.00	1-130	-	-
MEK Hussey	1	0	2	0	-	-	-	-
MJ Clarke	3.2	0	13	0	-	-	-	-
SPD Smith	31	3	138	0	-	-	-	-

Ryan Harris (below left) topped Australia's bowling averages, his 11 wickets costing only 25.54 apiece before injury struck. His best figures of six for 47 came in the solitary Australian victory in Perth.

Mike Hussey (below) was one of the few successes of Australia's batting line-up, comfortably topping the averages with 570 runs at 63.33. His two centuries included a 195 in the first Test at Brisbane.

126

ENGLAND SERIES AVERAGES

BATTING

	M	I	NO	R	HS	Avg	100	50	Ct	St
AN Cook	5	7	1	766	235*	127.66	3	2	5	-
IJL Trott	5	7	2	445	168*	89.00	2	1	1	-
IR Bell	5	6	1	329	115	65.80	1	3	3	-
KP Pietersen	5	6	0	360	227	60.00	1	1	5	-
MJ Prior	5	6	1	252	118	50.40	1	1	23	-
AJ Strauss	5	7	0	307	110	43.85	1	3	8	-
GP Swann	5	5	1	88	36*	22.00	-	-	6	-
TT Bresnan	2	2	0	39	35	19.50	-	-	-	-
PD Collingwood	5	6	0	83	42	13.83	-	-	9	-
CT Tremlett	3	4	1	19	12	6.33	-	-	-	-
JM Anderson	5	5	0	22	11	4.40	-	-	4	-
ST Finn	3	3	2	3	2	3.00	-	-	2	-
SCJ Broad	2	1	0	0	0	0.00	-	-	-	-

BOWLING

	O	M	R	W	Avg	Best	5 Wkt Inns	10 Wkt Match
KP Pietersen	5	0	16	1	16.00	1-10	-	-
TT Bresnan	82.4	25	215	11	19.54	4-50	-	-
CT Tremlett	122.3	28	397	17	23.35	5-87	1	-
JM Anderson	213.1	50	625	24	26.04	4-44	-	-
ST Finn	107.4	9	464	14	33.14	6-125	1	-
PD Collingwood	31	6	73	2	36.50	1-3	-	-
GP Swann	219.1	43	597	15	39.80	5-91	1	-
SCJ Broad	69.5	17	161	2	80.50	1-18	-	-

James Anderson (below) was England's leading wicket-taker with 24 victims, but occasional off-spinner Kevin Pietersen (below right) topped the tourists' bowling averages thanks to his solitary wicket, the crucial dismissal of Michael Clarke in Adelaide.

SERIES RECORDS

Top 10 Individual Scores

AN Cook	235*	England	Brisbane
KP Pietersen	227	England	Adelaide
MEK Hussey	195	Australia	Brisbane
AN Cook	189	England	Sydney
IJL Trott	168*	England	Melbourne
AN Cook	148	England	Adelaide
BJ Haddin	136	Australia	Brisbane
IJL Trott	135*	England	Brisbane
MJ Prior	118	England	Sydney
MEK Hussey	116	Australia	Perth

Top 10 Innings Bowling

MG Johnson	6/38	Australia	Perth
RJ Harris	6/47	Australia	Perth
PM Siddle	6/54	Australia	Brisbane
PM Siddle	6/75	Australia	Melbourne
ST Finn	6/125	England	Brisbane
CT Tremlett	5/87	England	Perth
GP Swann	5/91	England	Adelaide
CT Tremlett	4/26	England	Melbourne
JM Anderson	4/44	England	Melbourne
TT Bresnan	4/50	England	Melbourne

Top 10 Match Bowling

MG Johnson	9/82	Australia	Perth
RJ Harris	9/106	Australia	Perth
CT Tremlett	8/150	England	Perth
JM Anderson	7/127	England	Sydney
GP Swann	7/161	England	Adelaide
PM Siddle	6/75	Australia	Melbourne
TT Bresnan	6/75	England	Melbourne
JM Anderson	6/143	England	Adelaide
PM Siddle	6/144	Australia	Brisbane
ST Finn	6/150	England	Brisbane

Top 10 Team Totals

644	England	Sydney
620 for 5 dec	England	Adelaide
517 for 1 dec	England	Brisbane
513	England	Melbourne
481	Australia	Brisbane
309	Australia	Perth
304	Australia	Adelaide
281	Australia	Sydney
280	Australia	Sydney
268	Australia	Perth

10 Lowest Team Totals

98	Australia	Melbourne
123	England	Perth
187	England	Perth
245	Australia	Adelaide
260	England	Brisbane
268	Australia	Perth
280	Australia	Sydney
281	Australia	Sydney
304	Australia	Adelaide
309	Australia	Perth

Best Partnerships

1st wkt	England	188	AJ Strauss/AN Cook	Brisbane
2nd wkt	England	329*	AN Cook/IJL Trott	Brisbane
3rd wkt	England	175	AN Cook/KP Pietersen	Adelaide
4th wkt	Australia	113	SR Watson/MEK Hussey	Perth
5th wkt	England	116	KP Pietersen/IR Bell	Adelaide
6th wkt	Australia	307	MEK Hussey/BJ Haddin	Brisbane
7th wkt	England	107	IR Bell/MJ Prior	Sydney
8th wkt	England	102	MJ Prior/TT Bresnan	Sydney
9th wkt	Australia	76	MG Johnson/BW Hilfenhaus	Sydney
10th wkt	Australia	35	PM Siddle/BW Hilfenhaus	Perth

Top 10 Run-Scorers

		R	M
AN Cook	England	766	5
MEK Hussey	Australia	570	5
IJL Trott	England	445	5
SR Watson	Australia	435	5
KP Pietersen	England	360	5
BJ Haddin	Australia	360	5
IR Bell	England	329	5
AJ Strauss	England	307	5
MJ Prior	England	252	5
MJ Clarke	Australia	193	5

Top 10 Wicket-Takers

		W	M
JM Anderson	England	24	5
CT Tremlett	England	17	3
MG Johnson	Australia	15	4
GP Swann	England	15	5
ST Finn	England	14	3
PM Siddle	Australia	14	5
TT Bresnan	England	11	2
RJ Harris	Australia	11	3
BW Hilfenhaus	Australia	7	4
XJ Doherty	Australia	3	2

Top 10 Catches (excluding wicketkeepers)

		Ct	M
PD Collingwood	England	9	5
AJ Strauss	England	8	5
GP Swann	England	6	5
SR Watson	Australia	5	5
KP Pietersen	England	5	5
MEK Hussey	Australia	5	5
AN Cook	England	5	5
RT Ponting	Australia	4	4
JM Anderson	England	4	5
IR Bell	England	3	5

Leading Dismissals (wicketkeepers)

		Ct	St	M
MJ Prior	England	23	0	5
BJ Haddin	Australia	8	1	5